The Affirmation Handbook

Self-help, Volume 5

Timothy Scott Phillips

Published by Arcane Horizons Publishing, 2024.

THE AFFIRMATION HANDBOOK

First edition. November 28, 2024.

ISBN: 979-8230141914

Written by Timothy Scott Phillips.

Table of Contents

To those who dare to rewrite the stories they tell themselves,This book is for the dreamers, the strivers, and the believers in their own potential.

May these affirmations become your compass, guiding you toward the life you've always imagined.

Chapter 1: Introduction to Affirmations

Definition and History of Affirmations

Definition of Affirmations:

Affirmations are positive statements that individuals repeat to themselves regularly to challenge and overcome negative thoughts and self-sabotaging behaviors. They are tools used to reinforce desired beliefs and behaviors, helping to cultivate a positive mindset and encourage personal growth. The goal of affirmations is to reprogram the subconscious mind to encourage a more constructive and optimistic outlook on life.

Historical Background:

THE CONCEPT OF AFFIRMATIONS is not new. It has roots in various ancient philosophies and spiritual practices that recognized the power of spoken words. For example, mantras in Hinduism and Buddhism involve the repetition of sacred words or phrases to invoke spiritual growth and mental clarity. Similarly, prayers and affirmations in Christianity and Islam are used to foster faith and personal transformation.

In the modern era, the idea of affirmations gained prominence through the work of French psychologist Émile Coué in the early 20th century. Coué developed the method of conscious autosuggestion, which involved repeating positive statements to oneself to foster a positive mindset and facilitate healing. His famous affirmation, "Every day, in every way, I am getting better and better," has influenced many self-help and personal development practices.

The New Thought Movement, which emerged in the late 19th and early 20th centuries, also contributed to the popularization of affirmations. Prominent figures such as Ralph Waldo Emerson, James Allen, and Norman Vincent Peale advocated for the power of positive thinking and the use of affirmations to create a fulfilling life.

In recent decades, affirmations have become a staple in self-help literature, personal development programs, and therapeutic practices. Authors like Louise Hay, who wrote "You Can Heal Your Life," have brought affirmations to a wider audience, demonstrating their effectiveness in promoting mental, emotional, and physical well-being.

The Science Behind Affirmations and Their Impact on the Brain

NEUROPLASTICITY:

The science behind affirmations is grounded in the concept of neuroplasticity, which refers to the brain's ability to reorganize itself by forming new neural connections throughout life. Neuroplasticity allows the brain to adapt to new experiences, learn new information, and recover from injuries. When you repeatedly engage in a specific thought or behavior, you strengthen the neural pathways associated with that thought or behavior, making it more likely to occur in the future.

Affirmations leverage neuroplasticity by encouraging the repetition of positive statements, which can help to rewire the brain and replace negative thought patterns with more constructive ones. This process involves the activation of the brain's reward system, releasing neurotransmitters such as dopamine that promote feelings of well-being and motivation.

Self-Affirmation Theory:

SELF-AFFIRMATION THEORY, developed by social psychologist Claude Steele, posits that individuals can maintain their self-integrity by affirming their core values and beliefs. According to this theory, self-affirmation helps to reduce the impact of threats to self-identity, enhancing resilience and promoting adaptive coping strategies.

Research has shown that self-affirmation can buffer against stress, improve academic performance, and promote healthier behaviors. For example, studies have found that individuals who engage in self-affirmation are more likely to adhere to medical recommendations, exhibit lower levels of cortisol (a stress hormone), and demonstrate greater psychological resilience.

Cognitive Dissonance and Affirmations:

COGNITIVE DISSONANCE theory, proposed by Leon Festinger, suggests that individuals experience psychological discomfort when they hold conflicting beliefs or engage in behaviors that are inconsistent with their self-concept. This discomfort motivates individuals to reduce dissonance by changing their beliefs or behaviors to achieve consistency.

Affirmations can help to resolve cognitive dissonance by aligning one's thoughts and actions with their desired self-image. By consistently repeating positive affirmations, individuals can reduce the discrepancy between their current self-concept and their ideal self, fostering a sense of coherence and authenticity.

The Impact of Affirmations on the Brain:

AFFIRMATIONS ACTIVATE various regions of the brain associated with self-related processing, emotional regulation, and motivation. Functional magnetic resonance imaging (fMRI) studies have shown that engaging in self-affirmation activates the ventromedial prefrontal cortex (vmPFC), a brain region involved in self-referential thinking and the regulation of emotions. The activation of the vmPFC is associated with reduced defensive responses to threats and enhanced emotional resilience.

Moreover, affirmations can influence the brain's default mode network (DMN), which is involved in self-referential thinking and mind-wandering. By engaging in positive self-affirmation, individuals can modulate the activity of the DMN, promoting a more positive and constructive self-view.

Overview of How Affirmations Can Transform Your Mindset and Life

Cultivating a Positive Mindset:

AFFIRMATIONS PLAY A crucial role in cultivating a positive mindset by challenging and replacing negative thoughts with positive, empowering statements. A positive mindset is associated with numerous benefits, including increased resilience, improved mental health, and greater overall well-being.

Steps to Cultivate a Positive Mindset with Affirmations:

1. IDENTIFY NEGATIVE Thought Patterns: Begin by identifying the negative thoughts and beliefs that you want to change. These might include self-doubt, fear, or limiting beliefs about your abilities or worth.

2. Create Positive Affirmations: Craft positive affirmations that directly counteract your negative thoughts. Ensure that your affirmations are specific, present-tense, and reflect what you want to achieve or believe.

3. Repeat Affirmations Regularly: Integrate affirmations into your daily routine by repeating them consistently. This could be during your morning routine, before bedtime, or throughout the day.

4. Visualize Success: Combine affirmations with visualization techniques to enhance their effectiveness. Imagine yourself achieving your goals and embodying the qualities you affirm.

5. Stay Consistent: Consistency is key to reaping the benefits of affirmations. Make them a regular part of your self-care routine and remain patient as you work towards transforming your mindset.

Enhancing Self-Esteem and Confidence:

AFFIRMATIONS CAN SIGNIFICANTLY enhance self-esteem and confidence by reinforcing positive self-perceptions and encouraging self-acceptance. By focusing on your strengths and potential, affirmations help to build a more positive and empowering self-image.

Steps to Enhance Self-Esteem with Affirmations:

1. FOCUS ON STRENGTHS: Identify your strengths, achievements, and positive qualities. Create affirmations that highlight these aspects of yourself.

2. Affirm Self-Worth: Use affirmations to reinforce your inherent worth and value. Statements like "I am worthy of love and respect" or "I am enough just as I am" can be powerful.

3. Practice Self-Compassion: Incorporate self-compassionate affirmations that acknowledge your efforts and encourage self-kindness. For example, "I am doing my best, and that is enough."

4. Celebrate Progress: Regularly acknowledge and celebrate your progress, no matter how small. Affirmations like "I am proud of my achievements" can reinforce your confidence and self-esteem.

Promoting Mental and Emotional Well-Being:

AFFIRMATIONS CAN HAVE a profound impact on mental and emotional well-being by promoting positive emotions, reducing stress, and enhancing overall mood. They can serve as a tool for managing anxiety, depression, and other mental health challenges.

Steps to Promote Mental and Emotional Well-Being with Affirmations:

1. REDUCE STRESS: USE affirmations to manage stress and promote relaxation. Phrases like "I am calm and at peace" or "I handle stress with ease" can be helpful.

2. Encourage Positivity: Foster a positive outlook by affirming statements like "I choose to focus on the positive aspects of my life" or "I am grateful for the good things in my life."

3. Support Emotional Healing: Support emotional healing with affirmations that promote self-acceptance and forgiveness. For example, "I release past hurts and embrace healing" or "I am worthy of forgiveness and love."

4. Boost Mood: Enhance your mood with uplifting affirmations such as "I am filled with joy and gratitude" or "I radiate happiness and positivity."

Achieving Personal and Professional Goals:

AFFIRMATIONS CAN BE a powerful tool for achieving personal and professional goals by fostering a success-oriented mindset and enhancing motivation. By affirming your abilities and envisioning your success, you can create a positive trajectory toward your aspirations.

Steps to Achieve Goals with Affirmations:

1. SET CLEAR GOALS: Clearly define your personal and professional goals. Ensure that your affirmations align with these goals and reflect your desired outcomes.

2. Affirm Success: Use affirmations that reinforce your belief in your ability to achieve your goals. Statements like "I am capable of achieving great success" or "I am confident in my abilities" can boost motivation and determination.

3. Visualize Achievement: Combine affirmations with visualization techniques to create a vivid mental image of your success. Imagine yourself reaching your goals and experiencing the positive emotions associated with your achievements.

4. Stay Focused: Maintain focus and commitment by regularly repeating your affirmations. Use them as a reminder of your goals and the steps you need to take to achieve them.

Improving Relationships:

AFFIRMATIONS CAN ENHANCE relationships by promoting positive communication, empathy, and mutual respect. By affirming positive beliefs about yourself and others, you can create a more harmonious and supportive dynamic in your relationships.

Steps to Improve Relationships with Affirmations:

1. FOSTER EMPATHY: Use affirmations to cultivate empathy and understanding. Statements like "I listen with compassion and understanding" can enhance your ability to connect with others.

2. Encourage Positive Communication: Promote positive communication with affirmations that reinforce respectful and constructive interactions. For example, "I communicate openly and honestly" or "I express my feelings with kindness and respect."

3. Build Trust: Strengthen trust in your relationships with affirmations that emphasize reliability and integrity. Phrases like "I am trustworthy and dependable" can reinforce your commitment to building trust.

4. Enhance Connection: Use affirmations to deepen your connection with loved ones. Statements like "I cherish and nurture my relationships" or "I create meaningful connections with others" can foster a sense of closeness and support.

Conclusion

In this introductory chapter, we've explored the definition, history, and science behind affirmations, as well as their potential to transform your mindset and life. Affirmations are powerful tools that can help you cultivate a positive mindset, enhance self-esteem, promote mental and emotional well-being, achieve personal and professional goals, and improve relationships. By understanding the principles and benefits of affirmations, you are equipped to begin your journey toward a more empowered and fulfilling life.

As you continue reading this book, you will find practical techniques, inspiring stories, and additional insights to support your affirmation practice. Each chapter will provide you with the tools and encouragement you need to harness the power of affirmations and transform your mindset, ultimately leading to a life of greater joy, resilience, and success. Embrace this journey with an open heart and mind, and remember that the power to create positive change lies within you.

Chapter 2: The Power of Positive Thinking

Understanding the Role of Thoughts in Shaping Reality

The Nature of Thoughts:

Thoughts are the mental processes that occur in our minds, encompassing everything from fleeting images and ideas to deep reflections and problem-solving. They are a continuous stream of mental activity that influences our emotions, behaviors, and overall perception of reality. Understanding the power of our thoughts is essential because they can shape our experiences and outcomes in profound ways.

Cognitive-Behavioral Theory:

COGNITIVE-BEHAVIORAL theory (CBT) posits that our thoughts, feelings, and behaviors are interconnected. This framework suggests that the way we interpret and think about our experiences directly impacts our emotional responses and actions. For example, if you interpret a challenging situation as a personal failure, you may feel discouraged and give up. Conversely, if you see it as a learning opportunity, you may feel motivated to try again.

Self-Fulfilling Prophecies:

A SELF-FULFILLING PROPHECY occurs when our beliefs and expectations influence our behavior in ways that cause those beliefs to become reality. If you believe you will fail at a task, you may unconsciously act in ways that lead to failure, thereby confirming your initial belief. This concept underscores the importance of cultivating positive thoughts, as they can create a cycle of positive behaviors and outcomes.

The Law of Attraction:

THE LAW OF ATTRACTION is a philosophical concept suggesting that positive or negative thoughts bring positive or negative experiences into a person's life. It is based on the idea that thoughts are a form of energy, and positive energy attracts success, health, and happiness, while negative energy attracts the opposite. While scientifically unproven, many people find this concept empowering, encouraging them to focus on positive thoughts to attract positive outcomes.

Neuroscience and Thoughts:

NEUROSCIENCE RESEARCH shows that our thoughts can physically change the structure and function of our brains through a process called neuroplasticity. Repeated thoughts can strengthen neural pathways, making it easier for those thoughts to occur in the future. This means that regularly engaging in positive thinking can help rewire your brain to support a more optimistic and resilient mindset.

Thoughts and Perception:

OUR THOUGHTS ACT AS a lens through which we interpret and perceive the world. If you consistently think negatively, you are more likely to notice and focus on negative aspects of your experiences, reinforcing a pessimistic outlook. Conversely, positive thinking can shift your focus toward the positive aspects of life, enhancing your overall perception and experience of reality.

How Negative Thinking Affects Your Life

Impact on Mental Health:

NEGATIVE THINKING CAN have a detrimental impact on mental health. Persistent negative thoughts can contribute to conditions such as depression, anxiety, and chronic stress. These mental health issues can affect every aspect of your life, from your relationships and career to your physical health and overall well-being.

Cognitive Distortions:

NEGATIVE THINKING OFTEN involves cognitive distortions—irrational or exaggerated thought patterns that can reinforce negative emotions. Common cognitive distortions include:

- Catastrophizing: Expecting the worst possible outcome in any situation.

- Black-and-White Thinking: Viewing situations in extremes, with no middle ground.

- Overgeneralization: Drawing broad, negative conclusions based on a single event.

- Personalization: Blaming yourself for events outside your control.

- Filtering: Focusing only on the negative aspects of a situation while ignoring the positive.

Recognizing and challenging these distortions is a key step in overcoming negative thinking.

Impact on Physical Health:

NEGATIVE THINKING CAN also have a direct impact on physical health. Chronic stress and negative emotions can weaken the immune system, increase inflammation, and elevate the risk of conditions such as heart disease, high blood pressure, and diabetes. Additionally, negative thinking can lead to unhealthy behaviors, such as poor diet, lack of exercise, and substance abuse, further compromising physical health.

Effect on Relationships:

NEGATIVE THINKING CAN strain relationships by fostering mistrust, resentment, and conflict. If you frequently expect the worst from others or assume negative intentions, you may create a self-fulfilling prophecy that damages your relationships. Conversely, positive thinking can enhance relationships by promoting trust, empathy, and open communication.

Hindrance to Personal Growth:

NEGATIVE THINKING CAN hinder personal growth by creating a fear of failure and reducing motivation. If you believe you are incapable of achieving your goals or fear the consequences of trying, you may avoid taking risks and miss opportunities for growth and self-improvement. Positive thinking, on the other hand, encourages a growth mindset, where challenges are seen as opportunities for learning and development.

Career and Financial Impact:

IN THE WORKPLACE, NEGATIVE thinking can lead to decreased productivity, poor job performance, and strained relationships with colleagues. It can also hinder career advancement by undermining confidence and willingness to pursue new opportunities. Financially, negative thinking can lead to poor decision-making, increased risk aversion, and missed opportunities for wealth-building.

The Benefits of Cultivating a Positive Mindset

Enhanced Mental Health:

CULTIVATING A POSITIVE mindset can significantly improve mental health by reducing symptoms of depression, anxiety, and stress. Positive thinking promotes emotional resilience, helping you to cope better with life's challenges and setbacks. It also fosters a sense of optimism and hope, which are crucial for mental well-being.

Improved Physical Health:

A POSITIVE MINDSET can enhance physical health by reducing the negative impact of stress and promoting healthier behaviors. People with a positive outlook are more likely to engage in regular exercise, maintain a healthy diet, and avoid harmful habits such as smoking and excessive alcohol consumption. Additionally, positive thinking can boost the immune system and lower the risk of chronic diseases.

Better Relationships:

POSITIVE THINKING CAN improve relationships by fostering empathy, trust, and effective communication. When you approach interactions with a positive mindset, you are more likely to listen actively, understand others' perspectives, and resolve conflicts constructively. This creates stronger, more supportive relationships that enhance your overall quality of life.

Increased Motivation and Productivity:

A POSITIVE MINDSET can boost motivation and productivity by enhancing your belief in your abilities and encouraging a proactive approach to challenges. When you think positively, you are more likely to set ambitious goals, take initiative, and persevere in the face of obstacles. This can lead to greater success and fulfillment in both personal and professional endeavors.

Personal Growth and Development:

POSITIVE THINKING ENCOURAGES a growth mindset, where challenges are seen as opportunities for learning and improvement. This mindset fosters personal growth and development by promoting a willingness to take risks, embrace new experiences, and continuously strive for self-improvement. It also enhances self-esteem and confidence, which are crucial for achieving your goals.

Career Advancement:

IN THE WORKPLACE, A positive mindset can lead to better job performance, increased creativity, and stronger professional relationships. Positive thinkers are often seen as more adaptable, collaborative, and solution-oriented, making them valuable assets to any team. This can lead to career advancement and increased job satisfaction.

Financial Success:

CULTIVATING A POSITIVE mindset can also contribute to financial success. Positive thinkers are more likely to take calculated risks, pursue new opportunities, and make sound financial decisions. They are also better equipped to handle financial setbacks and maintain a long-term perspective on wealth-building.

Enhanced Resilience:

POSITIVE THINKING ENHANCES resilience by fostering a sense of control and empowerment. When you approach challenges with a positive mindset, you are more likely to see them as temporary and solvable, rather than insurmountable obstacles. This resilience enables you to bounce back from setbacks and continue moving forward.

Practical Strategies for Cultivating a Positive Mindset

1. Practicing Gratitude:

GRATITUDE IS A POWERFUL tool for shifting your focus from what is lacking in your life to what is abundant. Regularly practicing gratitude can enhance your overall sense of well-being and promote a positive mindset.

Steps for Practicing Gratitude:

1. KEEP A GRATITUDE Journal: Each day, write down three to five things you are grateful for. Reflect on the positive aspects of your life and express appreciation for them.

2. Express Gratitude to Others: Take time to thank the people in your life who have made a positive impact. Expressing gratitude strengthens relationships and fosters a sense of connection.

3. Focus on the Present Moment: Practice mindfulness to appreciate the present moment. Notice the small joys and positive experiences throughout your day.

2. Reframing Negative Thoughts:

REFRAMING INVOLVES challenging negative thoughts and replacing them with more positive and constructive perspectives. This cognitive restructuring can help break the cycle of negative thinking and promote a more optimistic outlook.

Steps for Reframing Negative Thoughts:

1. IDENTIFY NEGATIVE Thoughts: Pay attention to your internal dialogue and identify negative thoughts and cognitive distortions.

2. Challenge Negative Thoughts: Question the validity of negative thoughts and consider alternative perspectives. Ask yourself if there is evidence to support these thoughts or if they are based on irrational beliefs.

3. Replace with Positive Thoughts: Replace negative thoughts with positive affirmations and constructive perspectives. Focus on your strengths, accomplishments, and the potential for positive outcomes.

3. Engaging in Positive Self-Talk:

POSITIVE SELF-TALK involves using affirming and encouraging language when speaking to yourself. This practice can boost self-esteem, confidence, and overall well-being.

Steps for Engaging in Positive Self-Talk:

1. MONITOR YOUR SELF-Talk: Become aware of your internal dialogue and notice any negative or self-critical statements.

2. Replace Negative Self-Talk: Replace negative self-talk with positive affirmations and supportive statements. For example, change "I can't do this" to "I am capable and can handle this challenge."

3. Practice Regularly: Incorporate positive self-talk into your daily routine. Repeat affirmations regularly to reinforce positive beliefs.

4. Setting Realistic and Achievable Goals:

SETTING AND ACHIEVING goals can enhance your sense of purpose, motivation, and self-efficacy. Goals

provide direction and a sense of accomplishment, which can foster a positive mindset.

Steps for Setting Realistic and Achievable Goals:

1. DEFINE YOUR GOALS: Clearly define your personal and professional goals. Ensure they are specific, measurable, achievable, relevant, and time-bound (SMART).

2. Break Down Goals: Break down larger goals into smaller, manageable steps. This makes them more achievable and less overwhelming.

3. Track Progress: Regularly track your progress and celebrate milestones. Acknowledge your achievements and use them as motivation to continue moving forward.

5. Surrounding Yourself with Positive Influences:

THE PEOPLE AND ENVIRONMENTS you surround yourself with can significantly impact your mindset. Seek out positive influences that uplift and inspire you.

Steps for Surrounding Yourself with Positive Influences:

1. BUILD A SUPPORTIVE Network: Cultivate relationships with positive, supportive, and encouraging individuals. Engage with people who inspire you and contribute to your growth.

2. Create a Positive Environment: Create a living and working environment that promotes positivity. Surround yourself with uplifting books, music, and artwork.

3. Limit Exposure to Negativity: Limit your exposure to negative influences, such as toxic relationships, negative media, and environments that drain your energy.

6. Practicing Mindfulness and Meditation:

MINDFULNESS AND MEDITATION practices can enhance self-awareness, reduce stress, and promote a positive mindset. These practices encourage present-moment awareness and acceptance.

Steps for Practicing Mindfulness and Meditation:

1. START WITH SHORT Sessions: Begin with short mindfulness or meditation sessions, gradually increasing the duration as you become more comfortable.

2. Focus on the Breath: Use your breath as an anchor to bring your attention to the present moment. Notice the sensation of the breath entering and leaving your body.

3. Observe Without Judgment: Practice observing your thoughts, emotions, and sensations without judgment. Allow them to come and go without getting caught up in them.

4. Incorporate into Daily Life: Integrate mindfulness into your daily activities, such as eating, walking, and working. Pay attention to the present moment and engage fully in each experience.

7. Engaging in Physical Activity:

REGULAR PHYSICAL ACTIVITY is linked to improved mental health and a positive mindset. Exercise releases endorphins, which are natural mood enhancers, and promotes overall well-being.

Steps for Engaging in Physical Activity:

1. FIND ACTIVITIES You Enjoy: Choose physical activities that you enjoy, such as walking, running, dancing, or yoga. This increases the likelihood of consistency.

2. Set a Routine: Incorporate physical activity into your daily routine. Aim for at least 30 minutes of moderate exercise most days of the week.

3. Combine with Nature: Spend time in nature while engaging in physical activity. Nature has a calming effect and can enhance the positive impact of exercise.

8. Practicing Acts of Kindness:

ACTS OF KINDNESS, BOTH toward yourself and others, can boost your mood and promote a positive mindset. Kindness fosters a sense of connection and purpose.

Steps for Practicing Acts of Kindness:

1. PERFORM RANDOM ACTS of Kindness: Engage in small acts of kindness, such as complimenting a stranger, helping a neighbor, or volunteering your time.

2. Be Kind to Yourself: Practice self-compassion and self-care. Treat yourself with the same kindness and understanding that you would offer to a friend.

3. Reflect on Kindness: Reflect on the positive impact of your acts of kindness. Notice how they make you feel and the difference they make in others' lives.

Conclusion

In this chapter, we have explored the power of positive thinking and its profound impact on shaping reality. Understanding the role of thoughts, recognizing the detrimental effects of negative thinking, and cultivating a positive mindset are essential steps toward personal growth and well-being.

Positive thinking enhances mental and physical health, improves relationships, increases motivation and productivity, and fosters resilience and success.

By incorporating practical strategies such as practicing gratitude, reframing negative thoughts, engaging in positive self-talk, setting realistic goals, surrounding yourself with positive influences, practicing mindfulness, engaging in physical activity, and practicing acts of kindness, you can cultivate a positive mindset that transforms your life.

As you continue your journey, remember that positive thinking is a practice that requires consistency and commitment. Embrace the power of your thoughts, focus on the positive aspects of your experiences, and take intentional actions to foster a positive and empowering mindset. Your thoughts have the power to shape your reality, and by cultivating a positive mindset, you can create a life filled with joy, resilience, and fulfillment.

In the following chapters, we will delve deeper into specific areas where positive thinking and affirmations can make a significant impact, providing you with the tools and inspiration to transform your mindset and life.

Chapter 3: Crafting Effective Affirmations

Principles of Effective Affirmations

Crafting effective affirmations involves more than just repeating positive statements; it requires a thoughtful and strategic approach to ensure they resonate deeply and bring about meaningful change. Here are the foundational principles for creating powerful affirmations:

1. Positivity:

Effective affirmations are always stated in a positive manner. Instead of focusing on what you don't want, affirm what you do want. For example, rather than saying, "I don't want to be stressed," rephrase it to, "I am calm and relaxed."

2. Present Tense:

Affirmations should be stated in the present tense as if the desired outcome is already happening. This helps to trick the subconscious mind into believing that the affirmation is already true, which can lead to more immediate and impactful changes. For instance, use "I am confident" instead of "I will be confident."

3. Personal:

Affirmations should be personalized to reflect your individual goals, values, and desires. Use "I" statements to make the affirmation specific to you and your life. This personal touch makes the affirmation more relevant and powerful.

4. Specificity:

Being specific in your affirmations gives them more clarity and focus. Vague affirmations like "I am successful" are less effective than specific ones like "I am successful in my career and achieve my sales targets with ease."

5. Emotional Charge:

Incorporating emotion into your affirmations can amplify their effectiveness. Emotionally charged statements resonate more deeply with the subconscious mind. For example, "I feel joyous and grateful for my healthy body" is more impactful than simply "I am healthy."

6. Realism:

While affirmations should be positive and aspirational, they should also be realistic and believable. If an affirmation feels too far-fetched, it may create internal resistance. Start with affirmations that you can realistically believe, and as you progress, you can gradually expand your aspirations.

7. Repetition:

Consistency and repetition are key to embedding affirmations into your subconscious mind. Regularly repeating your affirmations helps to reinforce the desired beliefs and behaviors. This can be done through daily practice, using visual reminders, or integrating affirmations into your routine activities.

8. Clarity:

Clarity in affirmations helps avoid confusion and ensures that the subconscious mind receives a clear and precise message. Avoid using negative words or convoluted language. Keep your affirmations straightforward and to the point.

How to Write Powerful and Personalized Affirmations

WRITING POWERFUL AND personalized affirmations involves several steps to ensure they are tailored to your unique needs and goals. Here's a step-by-step guide to help you create effective affirmations:

1. Identify Your Goals and Desires:

BEGIN BY IDENTIFYING the areas of your life where you want to see change or improvement. These could include aspects such as career, relationships, health, personal growth, or financial success. Be clear about what you want to achieve.

Steps for Identifying Goals and Desires:

1. REFLECT ON YOUR Current Situation: Take some time to reflect on your current circumstances and identify areas where you feel dissatisfied or where you seek growth.

2. List Your Goals: Write down specific goals or desires you want to achieve. Be as detailed as possible to provide a clear focus for your affirmations.

3. Prioritize Your Goals: Determine which goals are most important to you and focus on creating affirmations for these areas first.

2. Turn Goals into Positive Statements:

ONCE YOU HAVE IDENTIFIED your goals, turn them into positive statements. Ensure that these statements reflect what you want to achieve rather than what you want to avoid.

Steps for Turning Goals into Positive Statements:

1. STATE IN THE POSITIVE: Reframe any negative or avoidance-based goals into positive affirmations. For example, instead of saying, "I don't want to feel anxious," say, "I am calm and at peace."

2. Use Present Tense: Write your affirmations in the present tense as if they are already true. This creates a sense of immediacy and helps to reinforce the desired belief.

3. Incorporate Emotion: Add an emotional component to your affirmations to make them more compelling. For instance, "I am confidently presenting my ideas at work and feeling proud of my contributions."

3. Make Affirmations Personal:

PERSONALIZE YOUR AFFIRMATIONS to ensure they resonate deeply with you. Use "I" statements and include specific details that reflect your individual circumstances and aspirations.

Steps for Personalizing Affirmations:

1. USE "I" STATEMENTS: Begin your affirmations with "I" to make them specific to you. For example, "I am achieving my financial goals" rather than "Financial goals are being achieved."

2. Include Specific Details: Add specific details that make your affirmations relevant to your life. For instance, "I am enjoying my daily morning runs in the park" is more personal than "I am exercising regularly."

3. Reflect Your Values: Ensure that your affirmations align with your core values and beliefs. This makes them more authentic and powerful.

4. Ensure Affirmations Are Realistic:

WHILE AFFIRMATIONS should be positive and aspirational, they should also be realistic and achievable. This helps to avoid creating internal resistance and enhances the likelihood of success.

Steps for Ensuring Realistic Affirmations:

1. ASSESS BELIEVABILITY: Evaluate whether your affirmations feel believable and achievable. If an affirmation feels too far-fetched, adjust it to make it more realistic.

2. Start Small: Begin with smaller, achievable affirmations and gradually build up to more ambitious ones as you gain confidence and experience.

3. Adjust as Needed: Be open to adjusting your affirmations based on your progress and changing circumstances. Flexibility ensures that your affirmations remain relevant and effective.

5. Create a Routine for Repetition:

REGULAR REPETITION is essential for embedding affirmations into your subconscious mind. Establish a routine that incorporates daily practice of your affirmations.

Steps for Creating a Routine for Repetition:

1. SET A SCHEDULE: Decide on specific times each day to practice your affirmations. This could be during your morning routine, before bedtime, or at designated times throughout the day.

2. Use Visual Reminders: Place visual reminders of your affirmations in prominent places, such as on your mirror, computer screen, or refrigerator. This helps to reinforce your affirmations throughout the day.

3. Incorporate into Activities: Integrate affirmations into routine activities, such as while exercising, commuting, or during breaks. This makes repetition easy and consistent.

6. Monitor and Reflect on Progress:

REGULARLY MONITOR AND reflect on your progress to assess the effectiveness of your affirmations. This helps to keep you motivated and make any necessary adjustments.

Steps for Monitoring and Reflecting on Progress:

1. KEEP A JOURNAL: Maintain a journal to track your progress and note any changes or improvements. Reflect on how your affirmations are impacting your thoughts, behaviors, and outcomes.

2. Celebrate Achievements: Acknowledge and celebrate your achievements, no matter how small. This reinforces positive behavior and keeps you motivated.

3. Adjust as Needed: Be open to revising your affirmations based on your progress and evolving goals. Flexibility ensures that your affirmations remain relevant and effective.

Examples of Well-Crafted Affirmations for Various Areas of Life

TO HELP YOU GET STARTED with crafting your own affirmations, here are examples of well-crafted affirmations for different areas of life. These examples follow the principles outlined above and can be personalized to fit your specific goals and circumstances.

1. Affirmations for Self-Love and Confidence:

- "I AM WORTHY OF LOVE and respect, and I honor my own needs and desires."

- "I am confident in my abilities and trust myself to make the right decisions."

- "I love and accept myself just as I am, and I am proud of my accomplishments."

2. Affirmations for Health and Wellness:

- "I AM HEALTHY, STRONG, and full of energy."

- "I nourish my body with wholesome foods and enjoy regular physical activity."

- "I am grateful for my body's ability to heal and thrive."

3. Affirmations for Career and Success:

- "I AM SUCCESSFUL IN my career and achieve my goals with ease and confidence."

- "I am open to new opportunities and trust in my ability to succeed."

- "I am a valuable and respected member of my team, and my contributions are appreciated."

4. Affirmations for Relationships:

- "I ATTRACT AND NURTURE loving, supportive, and healthy relationships."

- "I communicate openly and honestly with my loved ones, fostering trust and understanding."

- "I am surrounded by positive, uplifting people who bring out the best in me."

5. Affirmations for Financial Abundance:

- "I AM FINANCIALLY abundant and attract wealth and prosperity into my life."

- "I manage my finances wisely and make decisions that support my financial goals."

- "I am grateful for the financial resources I have and trust in my ability to create more."

6. Affirmations for Personal Growth and Development:

- "I AM CONSTANTLY GROWING and evolving, becoming the best version of myself."

- "I embrace challenges as opportunities for growth and learning."

- "I am committed to my personal development and take action toward my goals every day."

7. Affirmations for Overcoming Obstacles:

- "I AM RESILIENT AND capable of overcoming any challenge that comes my way."

- "I trust in my ability to navigate difficulties and emerge stronger and wiser."

- "I am resourceful and find creative solutions to any problem I encounter."

8. Affirmations for Creativity and Innovation:

- "I AM A CREATIVE AND innovative thinker, and my ideas are valuable and impactful."

- "I trust in my creative abilities and express myself freely and confidently."

- "I am open to new perspectives and embrace the flow of inspiration and creativity."

9. Affirmations for Spiritual Growth:

- "I AM CONNECTED TO my inner wisdom and trust in my spiritual journey."

- "I cultivate a sense of peace and harmony within myself and my surroundings."

- "I am open to receiving divine guidance and trust in the unfolding of my path."

10. Affirmations for Gratitude and Joy:

- "I AM GRATEFUL FOR the abundance of blessings in my life and focus on the positive."

- "I find joy in the simple pleasures of life and appreciate each moment fully."

- "I radiate happiness and positivity, and my joy is contagious to those around me."

Conclusion

Crafting effective affirmations is a powerful practice that can transform your mindset and, ultimately, your life. By following the principles of positivity, present tense, personalization, specificity, emotional charge, realism, repetition, and clarity, you can create affirmations that resonate deeply and bring about meaningful change.

The process of writing powerful and personalized affirmations involves identifying your goals, turning them into positive statements, making them personal, ensuring they are realistic, creating a routine for repetition, and monitoring your progress. Through regular practice, affirmations can help you cultivate self-love, enhance health and wellness, achieve career success, improve relationships, attract financial abundance, foster personal growth, overcome obstacles, boost creativity, support spiritual growth, and cultivate gratitude and joy.

As you continue to integrate affirmations into your daily life, remember that consistency and commitment are key to their effectiveness. Embrace this practice with an open heart and mind, and be patient with yourself as you work toward transforming your mindset. With dedication and perseverance, affirmations can become a powerful tool for creating a more positive, empowered, and fulfilling life.

In the following chapters, we will explore specific techniques, strategies, and inspiring stories to further support your affirmation practice and help you harness the full potential of positive thinking.

Chapter 4: Daily Affirmation Practices

Incorporating Affirmations into Your Daily Routine

Incorporating affirmations into your daily routine can transform your mindset and overall well-being. Regular practice is key to making affirmations effective, as consistency helps embed these positive statements into your subconscious mind. Here are several strategies for integrating affirmations into various aspects of your daily life:

1. Morning Affirmations:

STARTING YOUR DAY WITH affirmations sets a positive tone and mindset for the day ahead. Morning affirmations can help you focus on your goals, boost your confidence, and create a sense of gratitude.

Steps for Morning Affirmations:

1. CREATE A MORNING Ritual: Dedicate a few minutes each morning to your affirmation practice. Find a quiet space where you can focus without distractions.

2. Use a Mirror: Stand in front of a mirror and repeat your affirmations out loud. Making eye contact with yourself can enhance the impact of your affirmations.

3. Combine with Stretching or Yoga: Integrate affirmations into your morning stretching or yoga routine. As you move through each pose, repeat your affirmations to reinforce a positive mindset.

4. Visualize Your Day: As you repeat your affirmations, visualize how you want your day to unfold. Imagine yourself achieving your goals, interacting positively with others, and feeling confident and empowered.

Example Morning Affirmations:

- "I AM CONFIDENT, CAPABLE, and ready to take on the day."

- "I am grateful for this new day and the opportunities it brings."

- "I am filled with energy, vitality, and positivity."

2. Affirmations During Daily Activities:

INCORPORATING AFFIRMATIONS into routine activities throughout the day can help reinforce positive thinking and keep you focused on your goals.

Steps for Integrating Affirmations into Daily Activities:

1. WHILE COMMUTING: Use your commute as an opportunity to repeat your affirmations. If you drive, say them out loud or silently in your mind. If you use public transportation, listen to a recorded version of your affirmations on your phone.

2. During Exercise: Repeat your affirmations during your workout. Whether you're running, lifting weights, or doing yoga, affirmations can boost your motivation and enhance your focus.

3. At Work: Take short breaks throughout your workday to repeat your affirmations. This can help reduce stress, increase productivity, and maintain a positive mindset.

4. During Household Chores: Use time spent on household chores, such as cooking, cleaning, or gardening, to repeat your affirmations. These activities provide a perfect backdrop for reinforcing positive thoughts.

Example Affirmations for Daily Activities:

- "I AM FOCUSED, PRODUCTIVE, and accomplish my tasks with ease."

- "I am strong, healthy, and my body is capable of great things."

- "I bring positivity and enthusiasm to everything I do."

3. Evening Affirmations:

ENDING YOUR DAY WITH affirmations can help you reflect on your accomplishments, release any negative thoughts, and cultivate a sense of gratitude and peace.

Steps for Evening Affirmations:

1. CREATE AN EVENING Ritual: Dedicate a few minutes each evening to your affirmation practice. Find a calm and peaceful space where you can unwind and focus.

2. Reflect on Your Day: Reflect on the positive aspects of your day and acknowledge your achievements. Use your affirmations to reinforce these positive experiences.

3. Practice Gratitude: Include affirmations that express gratitude for the day's events, no matter how small. Gratitude helps shift your focus from what went wrong to what went right.

4. Prepare for Rest: Use affirmations that promote relaxation and prepare your mind for restful sleep. Calm and soothing affirmations can help you release any tension or stress from the day.

Example Evening Affirmations:

- "I AM PROUD OF WHAT I accomplished today and grateful for all the positive experiences."

- "I release any stress or tension from my body and mind, and I am at peace."

- "I am grateful for this day and look forward to a restful and restorative sleep."

Techniques for Repetition and Consistency

REPETITION AND CONSISTENCY are crucial for the effectiveness of affirmations. Regular practice helps to embed affirmations into your subconscious mind, making positive thinking a natural part of your daily life. Here are several techniques to ensure you repeat your affirmations consistently:

1. Setting Reminders:

USING REMINDERS CAN help you remember to practice your affirmations regularly. These reminders can be visual, auditory, or digital.

Steps for Setting Reminders:

1. USE VISUAL CUES: Place sticky notes with your affirmations in prominent places, such as on your mirror, refrigerator, or computer screen. These visual cues will remind you to repeat your affirmations throughout the day.

2. Set Alarms: Set alarms or notifications on your phone to remind you to practice your affirmations. Choose times when you can take a short break and focus on your affirmations.

3. Create Affirmation Cards: Write your affirmations on index cards and carry them with you. Review the cards whenever you have a few moments, such as while waiting in line or during a break.

2. Recording and Listening:

RECORDING YOUR AFFIRMATIONS and listening to them can be a powerful way to reinforce positive thinking. Hearing your affirmations in your own voice can make them more impactful.

Steps for Recording and Listening:

1. RECORD YOUR AFFIRMATIONS: Use a voice recorder or a recording app on your phone to record yourself repeating your affirmations. Speak clearly and with conviction.

2. Listen Regularly: Play the recordings while you're commuting, exercising, or relaxing. Listening to your affirmations can help reinforce them, especially if you find it challenging to repeat them out loud.

3. Create a Playlist: Combine your affirmation recordings with uplifting music to create a playlist. Listen to this playlist regularly to reinforce a positive mindset.

3. Using Affirmation Apps:

THERE ARE SEVERAL APPS designed to help you practice affirmations consistently. These apps can provide reminders, guided sessions, and tracking features.

Steps for Using Affirmation Apps:

1. CHOOSE AN APP: RESEARCH and choose an affirmation app that suits your needs. Look for features such as reminders, customization options, and guided sessions.

2. Set Up Reminders: Use the app to set up daily reminders to practice your affirmations. Schedule these reminders at times that fit your routine.

3. Track Progress: Many apps allow you to track your progress and see how consistent you've been with your practice. Use this feature to stay motivated and committed.

4. Partnering with an Accountability Buddy:

PARTNERING WITH AN accountability buddy can help you stay consistent with your affirmation practice. This person can provide encouragement and support.

Steps for Partnering with an Accountability Buddy:

1. CHOOSE A BUDDY: Choose a friend, family member, or colleague who is also interested in practicing affirmations. Agree to support each other in your practice.

2. Set Goals: Set specific goals for your affirmation practice and share them with your buddy. For example, you might agree to practice affirmations together every morning.

3. Check-In Regularly: Schedule regular check-ins to discuss your progress, share experiences, and provide encouragement. This could be through phone calls, video chats, or in-person meetings.

5. Creating a Dedicated Affirmation Space:

HAVING A DEDICATED space for your affirmation practice can enhance consistency and create a positive environment for reinforcing your affirmations.

Steps for Creating a Dedicated Affirmation Space:

1. CHOOSE A LOCATION: Choose a quiet and comfortable location in your home where you can practice your affirmations without distractions.

2. Personalize the Space: Decorate the space with items that inspire you, such as motivational quotes, calming images, or objects that bring you joy.

3. Keep Affirmation Tools Handy: Keep your affirmation cards, journal, and any other tools you use for your practice in this space. Having everything in one place makes it easier to maintain your routine.

Morning and Evening Affirmation Rituals

ESTABLISHING MORNING and evening affirmation rituals can enhance the effectiveness of your practice and create a positive framework for your day. These rituals can help you start your day with intention and end it with reflection and gratitude.

Morning Affirmation Rituals:

1. The Sunrise Routine:

BEGIN YOUR DAY WITH a ritual that harnesses the energy and potential of the morning. This routine can set a positive tone for the entire day.

Steps for the Sunrise Routine:

1. WAKE UP EARLY: SET your alarm to wake up early, allowing yourself some quiet time before the day begins.

2. Drink Water: Start your day by hydrating your body. Drinking a glass of water can help wake you up and prepare you for your affirmation practice.

3. Find a Quiet Space: Find a quiet and comfortable space where you can sit or stand without distractions.

4. Practice Deep Breathing: Take a few deep breaths to center yourself and clear your mind.

5. Repeat Affirmations: Repeat your morning affirmations out loud or silently in your mind. Use a mirror if possible to enhance the impact.

6. Visualize Your Day: Visualize your day unfolding positively, with you achieving your goals and interacting with others confidently and kindly.

7. Express Gratitude: End your ritual by expressing gratitude for the new day and the opportunities it brings.

Example Sunrise Routine Affirmations:

- "I AM GRATEFUL FOR this new day and the opportunities it brings."

- "I am confident, capable, and ready to take on the day."

- "I approach today with a positive attitude and an open heart."

2. The Empowerment Routine:

THE EMPOWERMENT ROUTINE focuses on boosting your confidence and motivation, preparing you to tackle the day's challenges with a positive mindset.

Steps for the Empowerment Routine:

1. WAKE UP WITH INTENTION: Set your alarm to a motivating song or sound that energizes you.

2. Stretch and Move: Begin your day with gentle stretching or a short workout to get your blood flowing and wake up your body.

3. Find Your Space: Find a quiet space where you can practice your affirmations without interruptions.

4. Use a Mirror: Stand in front of a mirror and make eye contact with yourself as you repeat your affirmations.

5. Speak with Conviction: Speak your affirmations with confidence and conviction. Feel the power of your words as you say them.

6. Visualize Success: Visualize yourself achieving your goals and handling challenges with ease and grace.

7. Set Intentions: Set specific intentions for the day, such as being productive, staying positive, or practicing kindness.

Example Empowerment Routine Affirmations:

- "I AM STRONG, CAPABLE, and confident in my abilities."

- "I am open to new opportunities and trust in my ability to succeed."

- "I am focused, motivated, and achieve my goals with ease."

3. The Mindful Morning Routine:

THE MINDFUL MORNING Routine incorporates mindfulness and meditation to create a calm and centered start to your day.

Steps for the Mindful Morning Routine:

1. WAKE UP GENTLY: Set your alarm to a gentle sound or nature sounds to wake up peacefully.

2. Practice Mindful Breathing: Begin your day with a few minutes of mindful breathing to center yourself and clear your mind.

3. Find Your Space: Find a quiet space where you can sit comfortably and practice your affirmations.

4. Meditate: Spend a few minutes in meditation, focusing on your breath and bringing your awareness to the present moment.

5. Repeat Affirmations: Repeat your affirmations silently in your mind or out loud, feeling each word as you say it.

6. Visualize Calm: Visualize yourself moving through your day with calm and ease, handling any challenges with grace.

7. Express Gratitude: End your ritual by expressing gratitude for the new day and the peace and calm you feel.

Example Mindful Morning Routine Affirmations:

- "I AM CALM, CENTERED, and at peace."

- "I approach today with mindfulness and an open heart."

- "I am grateful for this moment and the opportunities it brings."

Evening Affirmation Rituals:

1. The Reflection Routine:

THE REFLECTION ROUTINE focuses on reflecting on your day, acknowledging your achievements, and expressing gratitude.

Steps for the Reflection Routine:

1. FIND A QUIET SPACE: Find a quiet and comfortable space where you can relax and focus on your affirmations.

2. Reflect on Your Day: Spend a few minutes reflecting on your day. Acknowledge your achievements, no matter how small, and any positive experiences.

3. Practice Deep Breathing: Take a few deep breaths to center yourself and release any tension from the day.

4. Repeat Affirmations: Repeat your evening affirmations silently in your mind or out loud. Focus on releasing any negative thoughts and reinforcing positive ones.

5. Express Gratitude: End your ritual by expressing gratitude for the day's events and the lessons learned.

6. Prepare for Rest: Use calming affirmations to prepare your mind and body for restful sleep.

Example Reflection Routine Affirmations:

- "I AM PROUD OF WHAT I accomplished today and grateful for the positive experiences."

- "I release any stress or tension from my body and mind, and I am at peace."

- "I am grateful for this day and look forward to a restful and restorative sleep."

2. The Gratitude Routine:

THE GRATITUDE ROUTINE focuses on expressing gratitude and ending the day on a positive note.

Steps for the Gratitude Routine:

1. FIND A QUIET SPACE: Find a quiet and comfortable space where you can relax and focus on your affirmations.

2. Practice Gratitude: Spend a few minutes reflecting on the things you are grateful for, including positive experiences, relationships, and personal achievements.

3. Repeat Affirmations: Repeat your evening affirmations silently in your mind or out loud, focusing on gratitude and positivity.

4. Write in a Gratitude Journal: Write down three to five things you are grateful for in a gratitude journal. Reflect on these positive aspects of your day.

5. Express Gratitude: End your ritual by expressing gratitude for the day and the people in your life.

6. Prepare for Rest: Use calming affirmations to prepare your mind and body for restful sleep.

Example Gratitude Routine Affirmations:

- "I AM GRATEFUL FOR the abundance of blessings in my life."

- “I am thankful for the love and support of the people in my life.”

- “I am grateful for this day and the lessons it brought.”

3. The Relaxation Routine:

THE RELAXATION ROUTINE focuses on winding down and preparing your mind and body for restful sleep.

Steps for the Relaxation Routine:

1. CREATE A CALMING Environment: Create a calming environment by dimming the lights, playing soft music, or using essential oils.

2. Practice Deep Breathing: Begin your ritual with a few minutes of deep breathing to relax your mind and body.

3. Find Your Space: Find a quiet and comfortable space where you can relax and focus on your affirmations.

4. Repeat Affirmations: Repeat your evening affirmations silently in your mind or out loud, focusing on relaxation and peace.

5. Visualize Calm: Visualize yourself in a peaceful and serene setting, feeling calm and relaxed.

6. Prepare for Rest: Use calming affirmations to prepare your mind and body for restful sleep.

Example Relaxation Routine Affirmations:

- “I AM CALM, RELAXED, and at peace.”

- “I release any stress or tension from my body and mind.”

- “I am grateful for this day and look forward to a restful and restorative sleep.”

Conclusion

Incorporating affirmations into your daily routine, using techniques for repetition and consistency, and establishing morning and evening affirmation rituals can transform your mindset and overall well-being. By dedicating time each day to practice your affirmations, you can reinforce positive thinking, boost your confidence, and create a sense of gratitude and peace.

Morning affirmation rituals, such as the Sunrise Routine, the Empowerment Routine, and the Mindful Morning Routine, set a positive tone for the day and help you start your day with intention and focus. Evening affirmation rituals, such as the Reflection Routine, the Gratitude Routine, and the Relaxation Routine, allow you to reflect on your day, express gratitude, and prepare for restful sleep.

Consistency and repetition are key to making affirmations effective. Techniques such as setting reminders, recording and listening, using affirmation apps, partnering with an accountability buddy, and creating a dedicated affirmation space can help you stay consistent and committed to your practice.

By integrating these practices into your daily life, you can harness the power of affirmations to transform your mindset, achieve your goals, and create a more positive, empowered, and fulfilling life.

In the following chapters, we will explore specific areas where affirmations can make a significant impact, providing you with the tools and inspiration to harness the full potential of positive thinking.

Chapter 5: Affirmations for Self-Love and Confidence

Building Self-Esteem and Self-Worth through Affirmations

Self-esteem and self-worth are the foundation of a positive self-image and overall well-being. Affirmations can play a crucial role in building and reinforcing these qualities. They help to challenge and replace negative beliefs with positive, empowering thoughts, ultimately transforming how you perceive yourself.

Understanding Self-Esteem and Self-Worth:

SELF-ESTEEM REFERS to your overall sense of value and self-respect. It influences how you perceive your abilities, relationships, and potential. Self-worth, on the other hand, is the intrinsic belief that you are valuable and deserving of love and respect, independent of external achievements or validation.

The Role of Affirmations in Building Self-Esteem and Self-Worth:

AFFIRMATIONS HELP TO reprogram your subconscious mind, replacing negative self-perceptions with positive beliefs. By regularly repeating affirmations, you can shift your mindset and cultivate a stronger sense of self-esteem and self-worth.

Steps for Building Self-Esteem and Self-Worth through Affirmations:

1. IDENTIFY NEGATIVE Beliefs:

Begin by identifying the negative beliefs and self-perceptions that undermine your self-esteem and self-worth. These may include thoughts like "I am not good enough," "I don't deserve love," or "I am a failure."

Steps for Identifying Negative Beliefs:

1. REFLECT ON YOUR Thoughts: Take some time to reflect on your internal dialogue and notice any recurring negative thoughts or beliefs.

2. Write Them Down: Write down these negative beliefs to bring them to your conscious awareness.

3. Examine Their Origins: Consider where these beliefs originated. Are they based on past experiences, external criticism, or unrealistic standards?

2. Create Positive Affirmations:

ONCE YOU HAVE IDENTIFIED your negative beliefs, create positive affirmations that directly counteract them. Ensure that these affirmations are specific, present-tense, and reflect what you want to believe about yourself.

Steps for Creating Positive Affirmations:

1. REFRAME NEGATIVE Beliefs: Reframe each negative belief into a positive affirmation. For example, if you believe "I am not good enough," reframe it to "I am worthy and capable."

2. Use Positive Language: Use positive language that affirms your value and abilities. Avoid using words like "not" or "don't."

3. Be Specific: Make your affirmations specific to your goals and desires. For instance, instead of saying "I am confident," say "I am confident in my ability to speak up and share my ideas."

Examples of Affirmations for Building Self-Esteem and Self-Worth:

- "I AM WORTHY OF LOVE and respect just as I am."
- "I am proud of who I am and what I have accomplished."
- "I am confident in my abilities and trust myself to make the right decisions."

3. Integrate Affirmations into Your Daily Routine:

Regular repetition is key to making affirmations effective. Integrate your affirmations into your daily routine to reinforce positive beliefs consistently.

Steps for Integrating Affirmations into Your Daily Routine:

1. MORNING RITUAL: Start your day with affirmations to set a positive tone. Repeat them while getting ready, during your morning commute, or as part of your morning meditation.

2. Throughout the Day: Use reminders, such as sticky notes or phone alarms, to practice affirmations throughout the day. Take short breaks to repeat your affirmations and refocus your mind.

3. Evening Reflection: End your day with affirmations to reinforce positive beliefs before sleep. Reflect on your accomplishments and use affirmations to acknowledge your worth and efforts.

4. Visualize Success:

VISUALIZATION CAN ENHANCE the impact of your affirmations. Imagine yourself embodying the qualities and achieving the outcomes you affirm. This helps to create a vivid mental image of success and reinforces your positive beliefs.

Steps for Visualizing Success:

1. FIND A QUIET SPACE: Find a quiet and comfortable space where you can relax and focus on your visualization.

2. Close Your Eyes: Close your eyes and take a few deep breaths to center yourself.

3. Visualize Your Affirmations: Visualize yourself living out your affirmations. See yourself as confident, capable, and worthy. Imagine how it feels to achieve your goals and embody these qualities.

4. Engage Your Senses: Engage your senses in the visualization. What do you see, hear, feel, and even smell in this scenario? The more vivid the visualization, the more powerful it becomes.

5. Seek Support:

BUILDING SELF-ESTEEM and self-worth can be challenging, especially if negative beliefs are deeply ingrained. Seek support from friends, family, or a therapist to help you navigate this journey.

Steps for Seeking Support:

1. TALK TO TRUSTED Individuals: Share your goals and affirmations with trusted friends or family members who can provide encouragement and support.

2. Join Support Groups: Consider joining support groups or online communities focused on self-esteem and personal growth. Sharing experiences and affirmations with others can provide additional motivation and insights.

3. Work with a Therapist: A therapist can help you explore and address underlying issues that impact your self-esteem and self-worth. They can also provide guidance on creating and practicing affirmations.

Overcoming Self-Doubt and Negative Self-Talk

SELF-DOUBT AND NEGATIVE self-talk are common barriers to building self-love and confidence. They can undermine your efforts and reinforce negative beliefs about yourself. Affirmations can help you overcome these challenges by promoting positive self-perception and resilience.

Understanding Self-Doubt and Negative Self-Talk:

SELF-DOUBT INVOLVES questioning your abilities, decisions, and worth. It can lead to hesitation, anxiety, and a lack of confidence. Negative self-talk is the internal dialogue that criticizes, judges, or belittles you. It often stems from past experiences, external criticism, or unrealistic standards.

The Role of Affirmations in Overcoming Self-Doubt and Negative Self-Talk:

AFFIRMATIONS HELP TO counteract self-doubt and negative self-talk by reinforcing positive beliefs and promoting self-compassion. Regular practice can shift your internal dialogue from criticism to encouragement, enhancing your overall confidence and self-love.

Steps for Overcoming Self-Doubt and Negative Self-Talk with Affirmations:

1. RECOGNIZE AND CHALLENGE Negative Thoughts:

The first step in overcoming self-doubt and negative self-talk is to recognize and challenge these thoughts. Awareness allows you to identify patterns and intervene with positive affirmations.

Steps for Recognizing and Challenging Negative Thoughts:

1. INCREASE AWARENESS: Pay attention to your internal dialogue and notice any negative thoughts or self-doubt that arise. Write them down to make them more tangible.

2. Examine Evidence: Challenge the validity of these thoughts by examining the evidence. Are they based on facts or assumptions? Are they influenced by past experiences or external opinions?

3. Reframe Negative Thoughts: Reframe negative thoughts into positive affirmations. For example, if you think "I can't do this," reframe it to "I am capable and can handle this challenge."

Examples of Affirmations to Counteract Self-Doubt and Negative Self-Talk:

- "I TRUST MYSELF AND my abilities to make the right decisions."

- "I am worthy of success and embrace opportunities with confidence."

- "I am kind to myself and acknowledge my strengths and achievements."

2. Practice Self-Compassion:

SELF-COMPASSION INVOLVES treating yourself with the same kindness and understanding that you would offer to a friend. Affirmations that promote self-compassion can help you overcome self-doubt and negative self-talk.

Steps for Practicing Self-Compassion with Affirmations:

1. ACKNOWLEDGE YOUR Feelings: Recognize and validate your feelings without judgment. Understand that self-doubt and negative self-talk are common and part of the human experience.

2. Use Compassionate Affirmations: Create affirmations that promote self-compassion and understanding. For example, "I am doing my best, and that is enough" or "I forgive myself for any mistakes and learn from them."

3. Practice Regularly: Integrate self-compassionate affirmations into your daily routine. Use them during moments of self-doubt or when you catch yourself engaging in negative self-talk.

Examples of Self-Compassionate Affirmations:

- "I AM KIND AND GENTLE with myself, and I treat myself with compassion."

- "I acknowledge my efforts and am proud of my progress, no matter how small."

- "I forgive myself for any mistakes and embrace them as opportunities for growth."

3. Build Resilience:

RESILIENCE IS THE ABILITY to bounce back from setbacks and challenges. Affirmations that promote resilience can help you overcome self-doubt and negative self-talk by fostering a positive and proactive mindset.

Steps for Building Resilience with Affirmations:

1. FOCUS ON STRENGTHS: Create affirmations that highlight your strengths and abilities. Remind yourself of past successes and how you overcame challenges.

2. Embrace Challenges: Use affirmations to reframe challenges as opportunities for growth and learning. For example, "I embrace challenges and use them to become stronger and wiser."

3. Cultivate a Growth Mindset: Affirmations that promote a growth mindset can enhance resilience. For instance, "I am always learning and growing, and I welcome new experiences."

Examples of Resilience-Building Affirmations:

- "I AM RESILIENT AND capable of overcoming any challenge that comes my way."

- "I embrace challenges as opportunities for growth and learning."

- "I trust in my ability to navigate difficulties and emerge stronger and wiser."

4. Surround Yourself with Positivity:

SURROUNDING YOURSELF with positive influences can help counteract self-doubt and negative self-talk. Affirmations, combined with a supportive environment, can reinforce positive beliefs and boost your confidence.

Steps for Surrounding Yourself with Positivity:

1. SEEK SUPPORTIVE Relationships: Cultivate relationships with positive, supportive, and encouraging individuals. Share your affirmations and goals with them.

2. Create a Positive Environment: Decorate your living and working spaces with positive quotes, affirmations, and inspiring images. This visual reinforcement can uplift your mood and mindset.

3. Engage in Positive Activities: Engage in activities that bring you joy, relaxation, and fulfillment. These activities can help you feel more positive and confident.

Examples of Affirmations for a Positive Environment:

- "I AM SURROUNDED BY positive and supportive people who uplift and inspire me."

- "I create a positive and nurturing environment that supports my growth."

- "I engage in activities that bring me joy and fulfillment."

Personal Stories of Transformation through Self-Love Affirmations

PERSONAL STORIES OF transformation can provide powerful inspiration and motivation. Here are a few real-life examples of individuals who have used self-love affirmations to overcome self-doubt, build confidence, and transform their lives.

1. Emma's Journey to Self-Worth:

EMMA STRUGGLED WITH low self-esteem and self-worth for many years. She constantly compared herself to others and felt inadequate in various aspects of her life. This negative self-perception affected her relationships, career, and overall well-being.

Emma's Affirmation Practice:

EMMA DECIDED TO USE affirmations to challenge her negative beliefs and build self-worth. She created a list of affirmations that resonated with her goals and desires, such as "I am worthy of love and respect just as I am," "I am proud of who I am and what I have accomplished," and "I trust myself and my abilities."

Steps Emma Took:

1. DAILY PRACTICE: Emma integrated her affirmations into her daily routine. She repeated them every morning and evening, as well as during moments of self-doubt.

2. Visualization: Emma visualized herself embodying her affirmations. She imagined feeling confident, respected, and proud of her achievements.

3. Self-Compassion: Emma practiced self-compassion by acknowledging her efforts and progress. She used affirmations like "I am kind and gentle with myself" to reinforce self-love.

4. Seeking Support: Emma shared her affirmations with close friends and sought their encouragement. She also joined a support group focused on building self-esteem.

Emma's Transformation:

OVER TIME, EMMA NOTICED significant changes in her self-perception and confidence. She began to believe in her worth and value, which positively impacted her relationships and career. Emma's transformation was a testament to the power of affirmations in building self-worth and overcoming self-doubt.

2. James's Confidence Boost:

JAMES HAD ALWAYS STRUGGLED with confidence, particularly in social and professional settings. He often felt nervous and unsure of himself, which held him back from pursuing opportunities and expressing his ideas.

James's Affirmation Practice:

DETERMINED TO OVERCOME his lack of confidence, James decided to use affirmations. He created affirmations that focused on boosting his confidence and self-assurance, such as "I am confident in my abilities and trust myself to make the right decisions," "I speak up and share my ideas with confidence," and "I am capable and worthy of success."

Steps James Took:

1. MORNING RITUAL: James started his day with a morning ritual that included repeating his affirmations in front of a mirror. He made eye contact with himself and spoke with conviction.

2. Throughout the Day: James used reminders on his phone to practice his affirmations throughout the day, especially before important meetings or social events.

3. Positive Visualization: James visualized himself confidently navigating social and professional situations. He imagined speaking clearly, making eye contact, and receiving positive feedback.

4. Accountability Buddy: James partnered with a friend who also wanted to build confidence. They checked in with each other regularly and provided mutual support.

James's Transformation:

AS JAMES CONTINUED his affirmation practice, he noticed a gradual increase in his confidence. He began to speak up more in meetings, share his ideas, and take on new challenges. James's enhanced confidence positively impacted his career and social life, demonstrating the effectiveness of affirmations in building self-assurance.

3. Lily's Path to Self-Love:

LILY HAD A HISTORY of negative self-talk and struggled with accepting herself. She often criticized her appearance, abilities, and decisions, which took a toll on her mental and emotional well-being.

Lily's Affirmation Practice:

LILY DECIDED TO USE affirmations to cultivate self-love and overcome negative self-talk. She created affirmations that focused on self-acceptance, kindness, and worthiness, such as "I love and accept myself just as I am," "I am worthy of love and respect," and "I am proud of my efforts and progress."

Steps Lily Took:

1. AFFIRMATION JOURNAL: Lily kept an affirmation journal where she wrote down her affirmations and reflected on their impact. She made it a daily habit to write and repeat her affirmations.

2. Gratitude Practice: Lily combined her affirmations with a gratitude practice. Each day, she wrote down three things she was grateful for, including aspects of herself she appreciated.

3. Mindful Meditation: Lily integrated affirmations into her meditation practice. She repeated her affirmations silently while meditating, focusing on their meaning and emotional resonance.

4. Positive Environment: Lily surrounded herself with positivity by decorating her living space with uplifting quotes, images, and reminders of her affirmations.

Lily's Transformation:

THROUGH CONSISTENT practice, Lily noticed a shift in her self-perception and inner dialogue. She became kinder and more compassionate toward herself, embracing her unique qualities and strengths. Lily's journey to self-love highlighted the transformative power of affirmations in overcoming negative self-talk and fostering self-acceptance.

4. David's Journey to Resilience:

DAVID FACED NUMEROUS challenges and setbacks in his life, leading to feelings of self-doubt and inadequacy. He often felt overwhelmed by difficulties and questioned his ability to overcome them.

David's Affirmation Practice:

DETERMINED TO BUILD resilience, David decided to use affirmations. He created affirmations that emphasized his strength, resourcefulness, and ability to navigate challenges, such as "I am resilient and capable of overcoming any challenge that comes my way," "I trust in my ability to navigate difficulties and emerge stronger," and "I embrace challenges as opportunities for growth and learning."

Steps David Took:

1. DAILY AFFIRMATION Routine: David integrated affirmations into his daily routine, repeating them every morning and evening. He also used affirmations during moments of stress or self-doubt.

2. Positive Visualization: David visualized himself successfully overcoming challenges and achieving his goals. He imagined feeling strong, resourceful, and triumphant.

3. Resilience Journal: David kept a resilience journal where he recorded his affirmations, reflected on his progress, and noted instances where he demonstrated resilience.

4. Support Network: David sought support from friends, family, and mentors who encouraged and uplifted him. He shared his affirmations and goals with them for additional motivation.

David's Transformation:

THROUGH HIS AFFIRMATION practice, David developed a stronger sense of resilience and self-assurance. He began to view challenges as opportunities for growth and approached difficulties with a positive mindset. David's transformation showcased the power of affirmations in building resilience and overcoming self-doubt.

Conclusion

Affirmations are powerful tools for building self-love and confidence. By challenging negative beliefs, promoting self-compassion, and reinforcing positive self-perceptions, affirmations can transform your mindset and overall well-being. The journey to self-love and confidence involves regular practice, self-awareness, and a commitment to positive change.

In this chapter, we explored how to build self-esteem and self-worth through affirmations, overcome self-doubt and negative self-talk, and shared personal stories of transformation. These stories demonstrate the profound impact affirmations can have on individuals' lives, providing inspiration and motivation for your own journey.

As you continue to integrate affirmations into your daily routine, remember to be patient and compassionate with yourself. Positive change takes time, but with consistency and dedication, you can cultivate self-love and confidence, leading to a more empowered and fulfilling life.

In the following chapters, we will explore specific areas where affirmations can make a significant impact, providing you with the tools and inspiration to harness the full potential of positive thinking.

Chapter 6: Affirmations for Health and Wellness

Promoting Physical Health Through Positive Affirmations

Affirmations can significantly impact physical health by fostering a positive mindset and encouraging healthy behaviors. By repeating positive statements about your body, health, and lifestyle, you can reinforce your commitment to well-being and create a more health-conscious mindset.

Understanding the Connection Between Mindset and Physical Health:

THE MIND-BODY CONNECTION is well-documented in scientific research. Positive thoughts and beliefs can influence physical health by reducing stress, boosting the immune system, and promoting healthy behaviors. Conversely, negative thoughts and stress can lead to a range of physical health issues, including weakened immunity, increased inflammation, and chronic conditions.

The Role of Affirmations in Promoting Physical Health:

AFFIRMATIONS CAN HELP you adopt a positive outlook on your health and well-being. They can encourage you to make healthier choices, stay committed to fitness goals, and maintain a positive attitude toward your body.

Steps for Promoting Physical Health Through Affirmations:

1. Identify Health Goals:

START BY IDENTIFYING your health goals. These could include losing weight, building muscle, improving cardiovascular health, or simply maintaining overall wellness.

Steps for Identifying Health Goals:

1. REFLECT ON YOUR Current Health: Assess your current health status and identify areas where you want to see improvement.

2. Set Specific Goals: Define clear and specific health goals. For example, "I want to lose 10 pounds in the next three months" or "I want to run a 5k race."

3. Prioritize Your Goals: Determine which goals are most important to you and focus on creating affirmations for these areas first.

2. Create Health-Focused Affirmations:

ONCE YOU HAVE IDENTIFIED your health goals, create affirmations that support these goals. Ensure that these affirmations are positive, specific, and reflect what you want to achieve.

Steps for Creating Health-Focused Affirmations:

1. REFRAME NEGATIVE Beliefs: Identify any negative beliefs you have about your health and reframe them into positive affirmations. For example, if you believe "I can't stick to a healthy diet," reframe it to "I enjoy eating nutritious foods that nourish my body."

2. Use Positive Language: Use positive language that affirms your health and wellness. Avoid using words like "not" or "don't."

3. Be Specific: Make your affirmations specific to your health goals. For instance, instead of saying "I am healthy," say "I am strong and full of energy because I exercise regularly."

Examples of Affirmations for Physical Health:

- "I AM HEALTHY, STRONG, and full of energy."

- "I nourish my body with wholesome foods and enjoy regular physical activity."

- "I am committed to maintaining a healthy lifestyle and taking care of my body."

3. Integrate Affirmations into Your Daily Routine:

Consistency is key to making affirmations effective. Integrate your health-focused affirmations into your daily routine to reinforce positive beliefs about your health.

Steps for Integrating Affirmations into Your Daily Routine:

1. MORNING RITUAL: Start your day with health-focused affirmations to set a positive tone. Repeat them while getting ready, during your morning commute, or as part of your morning meditation.

2. During Exercise: Repeat your affirmations during your workout. Whether you're running, lifting weights, or doing yoga, affirmations can boost your motivation and enhance your focus on health.

3. Meal Times: Use affirmations during meal times to reinforce healthy eating habits. For example, "I choose nutritious foods that nourish my body."

4. Evening Reflection: End your day with affirmations to reinforce positive beliefs before sleep. Reflect on your health goals and use affirmations to acknowledge your progress.

4. Visualize Optimal Health:

VISUALIZATION CAN ENHANCE the impact of your affirmations. Imagine yourself embodying the health and wellness you desire. This helps to create a vivid mental image of success and reinforces your positive beliefs.

Steps for Visualizing Optimal Health:

1. FIND A QUIET SPACE: Find a quiet and comfortable space where you can relax and focus on your visualization.

2. Close Your Eyes: Close your eyes and take a few deep breaths to center yourself.

3. Visualize Your Affirmations: Visualize yourself living out your health-focused affirmations. See yourself as strong, energetic, and vibrant. Imagine how it feels to achieve your health goals and embody these qualities.

4. Engage Your Senses: Engage your senses in the visualization. What do you see, hear, feel, and even smell in this scenario? The more vivid the visualization, the more powerful it becomes.

5. Seek Support:

BUILDING AND MAINTAINING physical health can be challenging, especially if you're working to overcome ingrained habits or health issues. Seek support from friends, family, or a health professional to help you stay motivated and committed.

Steps for Seeking Support:

1. TALK TO TRUSTED Individuals: Share your health goals and affirmations with trusted friends or family members who can provide encouragement and support.

2. Join Support Groups: Consider joining support groups or online communities focused on health and wellness. Sharing experiences and affirmations with others can provide additional motivation and insights.

3. Work with a Health Professional: A health professional can help you create a personalized plan for achieving your health goals and provide guidance on maintaining a healthy lifestyle.

Mental Health Benefits of Affirmations

MENTAL HEALTH IS A crucial component of overall well-being. Affirmations can significantly benefit mental health by promoting positive thinking, reducing stress, and enhancing emotional resilience.

Understanding the Impact of Affirmations on Mental Health:

AFFIRMATIONS WORK BY challenging and replacing negative thoughts with positive beliefs. This shift in mindset can reduce symptoms of anxiety and depression, boost self-esteem, and improve overall mental health.

The Role of Affirmations in Enhancing Mental Health:

AFFIRMATIONS CAN HELP you develop a more positive outlook, increase self-awareness, and cultivate a sense of inner peace and emotional stability.

Steps for Enhancing Mental Health Through Affirmations:

1. Identify Mental Health Goals:

START BY IDENTIFYING your mental health goals. These could include reducing anxiety, managing depression, increasing self-esteem, or enhancing emotional resilience.

Steps for Identifying Mental Health Goals:

1. REFLECT ON YOUR Current Mental Health: Assess your current mental health status and identify areas where you want to see improvement.

2. Set Specific Goals: Define clear and specific mental health goals. For example, "I want to reduce my anxiety levels" or "I want to feel more confident in social situations."

3. Prioritize Your Goals: Determine which goals are most important to you and focus on creating affirmations for these areas first.

2. Create Mental Health-Focused Affirmations:

ONCE YOU HAVE IDENTIFIED your mental health goals, create affirmations that support these goals. Ensure that these affirmations are positive, specific, and reflect what you want to achieve.

Steps for Creating Mental Health-Focused Affirmations:

1. REFRAME NEGATIVE Beliefs: Identify any negative beliefs you have about your mental health and reframe them into positive affirmations. For example, if you believe "I am always anxious," reframe it to "I am calm and at peace."

2. Use Positive Language: Use positive language that affirms your mental health and well-being. Avoid using words like "not" or "don't."

3. Be Specific: Make your affirmations specific to your mental health goals. For instance, instead of saying "I am happy," say "I feel joy and gratitude in my daily life."

Examples of Affirmations for Mental Health:

- "I AM CALM, CENTERED, and at peace."

- "I trust in my ability to manage my emotions and maintain my mental health."

- "I am worthy of love, respect, and happiness."

3. Integrate Affirmations into Your Daily Routine:

CONSISTENCY IS KEY to making affirmations effective. Integrate your mental health-focused affirmations into your daily routine to reinforce positive beliefs about your mental well-being.

Steps for Integrating Affirmations into Your Daily Routine:

1. MORNING RITUAL: Start your day with mental health-focused affirmations to set a positive tone. Repeat them while getting ready, during your morning commute, or as part of your morning meditation.

2. Throughout the Day: Use reminders, such as sticky notes or phone alarms, to practice your affirmations throughout the day. Take short breaks to repeat your affirmations and refocus your mind.

3. Evening Reflection: End your day with affirmations to reinforce positive beliefs before sleep. Reflect on your mental health goals and use affirmations to acknowledge your progress.

4. Visualize Mental Well-Being:

VISUALIZATION CAN ENHANCE the impact of your affirmations. Imagine yourself embodying the mental health and well-being you desire. This helps to create a vivid mental image of success and reinforces your positive beliefs.

Steps for Visualizing Mental Well-Being:

1. FIND A QUIET SPACE: Find a quiet and comfortable space where you can relax and focus on your visualization.

2. Close Your Eyes: Close your eyes and take a few deep breaths to center yourself.

3. Visualize Your Affirmations: Visualize yourself living out your mental health-focused affirmations. See yourself as calm, centered, and emotionally resilient. Imagine how it feels to achieve your mental health goals and embody these qualities.

4. Engage Your Senses: Engage your senses in the visualization. What do you see, hear, feel, and even smell in this scenario? The more vivid the visualization, the more powerful it becomes.

5. Practice Mindfulness:

MINDFULNESS IS THE practice of being present and fully engaged in the current moment. Integrating mindfulness with affirmations can enhance your mental health by promoting awareness and reducing stress.

Steps for Practicing Mindfulness with Affirmations:

1. MINDFUL BREATHING: Combine affirmations with mindful breathing exercises. As you inhale, repeat a calming affirmation like "I am calm and at peace." As you exhale, release any tension or stress.

2. Mindful Meditation: Integrate affirmations into your meditation practice. Repeat your affirmations silently while meditating, focusing on their meaning and emotional resonance.

3. Mindful Activities: Practice affirmations during mindful activities such as walking, eating, or listening to music. Stay present and fully engage in the activity while repeating your affirmations.

Examples of Mindfulness-Integrated Affirmations:

- "I AM FULLY PRESENT and engaged in this moment."

- "I am aware of my thoughts and emotions, and I choose peace."

- "I am grateful for the present moment and the calm it brings."

Affirmations for Stress Reduction and Overall Well-Being

STRESS IS A COMMON issue that can negatively impact both mental and physical health. Affirmations can be a powerful tool for reducing stress and promoting overall well-being by encouraging a calm, positive, and balanced mindset.

Understanding the Impact of Stress on Health:

CHRONIC STRESS CAN lead to a range of health issues, including anxiety, depression, heart disease, digestive problems, and weakened immunity. Managing stress is essential for maintaining overall well-being and quality of life.

The Role of Affirmations in Reducing Stress:

AFFIRMATIONS CAN HELP manage stress by promoting relaxation, reducing negative thinking, and fostering a positive outlook. Regular practice can enhance your ability to cope with stress and maintain emotional balance.

Steps for Reducing Stress and Promoting Well-Being Through Affirmations:

1. Identify Stressors:

START BY IDENTIFYING the primary sources of stress in your life. These could include work, relationships, financial concerns, or health issues.

Steps for Identifying Stressors:

1. REFLECT ON YOUR Life: Take some time to reflect on different areas of your life and identify what causes you the most stress.

2. Write Them Down: Write down these stressors to bring them to your conscious awareness.

3. Assess Their Impact Consider how each stressor affects your mental, emotional, and physical health.

2. Create Stress-Reduction Affirmations:

ONCE YOU HAVE IDENTIFIED your stressors, create affirmations that promote relaxation, calm, and emotional balance. Ensure that these affirmations are positive, specific, and reflect what you want to achieve.

Steps for Creating Stress-Reduction Affirmations:

1. REFRAME NEGATIVE Beliefs: Identify any negative beliefs you have about stress and reframe them into positive affirmations. For example, if you believe "I can't handle this stress," reframe it to "I am capable of managing stress with ease."

2. Use Positive Language: Use positive language that affirms your ability to cope with stress and maintain well-being. Avoid using words like "not" or "don't."

3. Be Specific: Make your affirmations specific to your stress reduction goals. For instance, instead of saying "I am relaxed," say "I feel calm and relaxed in challenging situations."

Examples of Affirmations for Stress Reduction:

- "I AM CALM, RELAXED, and in control."

- "I handle stress with ease and maintain my emotional balance."

- "I am grateful for the peace and calm in my life."

3. Integrate Affirmations into Your Daily Routine:

CONSISTENCY IS KEY to making affirmations effective. Integrate your stress-reduction affirmations into your daily routine to reinforce positive beliefs about your ability to manage stress.

Steps for Integrating Affirmations into Your Daily Routine:

1. MORNING RITUAL: Start your day with stress-reduction affirmations to set a positive tone. Repeat them while getting ready, during your morning commute, or as part of your morning meditation.

2. During Stressful Moments: Use affirmations during moments of stress to calm your mind and body. Take a few deep breaths and repeat your affirmations to regain composure.

3. Evening Reflection: End your day with affirmations to release any accumulated stress and promote relaxation before sleep. Reflect on your stress reduction goals and use affirmations to acknowledge your progress.

4. Visualize Calm and Peace:

VISUALIZATION CAN ENHANCE the impact of your affirmations. Imagine yourself embodying the calm and peace you desire. This helps to create a vivid mental image of relaxation and reinforces your positive beliefs.

Steps for Visualizing Calm and Peace:

1. FIND A QUIET SPACE: Find a quiet and comfortable space where you can relax and focus on your visualization.

2. Close Your Eyes: Close your eyes and take a few deep breaths to center yourself.

3. Visualize Your Affirmations: Visualize yourself living out your stress-reduction affirmations. See yourself as calm, relaxed, and in control. Imagine how it feels to manage stress with ease and maintain emotional balance.

4. Engage Your Senses: Engage your senses in the visualization. What do you see, hear, feel, and even smell in this scenario? The more vivid the visualization, the more powerful it becomes.

5. Practice Relaxation Techniques:

INTEGRATING AFFIRMATIONS with relaxation techniques can enhance their effectiveness in reducing stress and promoting overall well-being.

Steps for Practicing Relaxation Techniques with Affirmations:

1. Deep Breathing: Combine affirmations with deep breathing exercises. As you inhale, repeat a calming affirmation like "I am calm and at peace." As you exhale, release any tension or stress.

2. Progressive Muscle Relaxation: Use affirmations during progressive muscle relaxation. Tense and relax different muscle groups while repeating affirmations like "I release all tension from my body and mind."

3. Guided Imagery: Integrate affirmations with guided imagery exercises. Imagine yourself in a peaceful and serene setting while repeating affirmations like "I am surrounded by calm and tranquility."

Examples of Affirmations for Relaxation Techniques:

- "I AM CALM, RELAXED, and in control."

- "I release all tension from my body and mind."

- "I am surrounded by peace and tranquility."

Conclusion

Affirmations are powerful tools for promoting health and wellness. By fostering a positive mindset and encouraging healthy behaviors, affirmations can significantly impact physical and mental health, reduce stress, and enhance overall well-being.

In this chapter, we explored how to promote physical health through positive affirmations, the mental health benefits of affirmations, and how to use affirmations for stress reduction and overall well-being. By integrating affirmations into your daily routine, creating specific and positive affirmations, and combining them with visualization and relaxation techniques, you can cultivate a healthier and more balanced life.

As you continue to practice affirmations for health and wellness, remember to be patient and consistent. Positive change takes time, but with dedication and perseverance, you can harness the power of affirmations to transform your health and well-being.

In the following chapters, we will explore specific areas where affirmations can make a significant impact, providing you with the tools and inspiration to harness the full potential of positive thinking.

Chapter 7: Affirmations for Career and Success

Enhancing Career Growth and Professional Development

Affirmations can be powerful tools to enhance career growth and professional development. They help cultivate a positive mindset, increase motivation, and reinforce your commitment to achieving your career goals. By regularly practicing affirmations, you can overcome self-doubt, build confidence, and create a clear vision for your professional future.

Understanding the Role of Mindset in Career Success:

YOUR MINDSET SIGNIFICANTLY influences your career trajectory. A positive mindset can boost your confidence, resilience, and willingness to take on challenges, while a negative mindset can hinder your progress and lead to self-sabotaging behaviors. Affirmations help shift your mindset towards positivity, enabling you to embrace opportunities and achieve your professional aspirations.

The Role of Affirmations in Enhancing Career Growth:

AFFIRMATIONS CAN HELP you:

- Build confidence in your skills and abilities

- Set and achieve career goals

- Maintain motivation and focus

- Overcome obstacles and setbacks

- Foster a proactive and growth-oriented mindset

Steps for Enhancing Career Growth Through Affirmations:

1. Identify Career Goals:

BEGIN BY IDENTIFYING your career goals. These could include short-term objectives like completing a project or long-term aspirations like advancing to a leadership position.

Steps for Identifying Career Goals:

1. REFLECT ON YOUR Career: Assess your current career situation and identify areas where you want to see growth or change.

2. Set Specific Goals: Define clear and specific career goals. For example, "I want to improve my leadership skills" or "I want to secure a promotion within the next year."

3. Prioritize Your Goals: Determine which goals are most important to you and focus on creating affirmations for these areas first.

2. Create Career-Focused Affirmations:

ONCE YOU HAVE IDENTIFIED your career goals, create affirmations that support these goals. Ensure that these affirmations are positive, specific, and reflect what you want to achieve.

Steps for Creating Career-Focused Affirmations:

1. REFRAME NEGATIVE Beliefs: Identify any negative beliefs you have about your career and reframe them into positive affirmations. For example, if you believe "I am not qualified for a leadership role," reframe it to "I have the skills and qualities to be an effective leader."

2. Use Positive Language: Use positive language that affirms your career growth and success. Avoid using words like "not" or "don't."

3. Be Specific: Make your affirmations specific to your career goals. For instance, instead of saying "I am successful," say "I am successful in my career and achieve my professional goals with ease."

Examples of Affirmations for Career Growth:

- "I AM CONFIDENT IN my skills and abilities and use them to achieve my career goals."

- "I am proactive and take initiative to advance my career."

- "I am open to new opportunities and trust in my ability to succeed."

3. Integrate Affirmations into Your Daily Routine:

CONSISTENCY IS KEY to making affirmations effective. Integrate your career-focused affirmations into your daily routine to reinforce positive beliefs about your professional growth.

Steps for Integrating Affirmations into Your Daily Routine:

1. MORNING RITUAL: Start your day with career-focused affirmations to set a positive tone. Repeat them while getting ready, during your morning commute, or as part of your morning meditation.

2. At Work: Use reminders, such as sticky notes or phone alarms, to practice your affirmations throughout the workday. Take short breaks to repeat your affirmations and refocus your mind.

3. Evening Reflection: End your day with affirmations to reinforce positive beliefs before sleep. Reflect on your career goals and use affirmations to acknowledge your progress.

4. Visualize Career Success:

VISUALIZATION CAN ENHANCE the impact of your affirmations. Imagine yourself achieving your career goals and embodying the qualities you affirm. This helps to create a vivid mental image of success and reinforces your positive beliefs.

Steps for Visualizing Career Success:

1. FIND A QUIET SPACE: Find a quiet and comfortable space where you can relax and focus on your visualization.

2. Close Your Eyes: Close your eyes and take a few deep breaths to center yourself.

3. Visualize Your Affirmations: Visualize yourself living out your career-focused affirmations. See yourself as confident, successful, and fulfilled in your professional role. Imagine how it feels to achieve your career goals and embody these qualities.

4. Engage Your Senses: Engage your senses in the visualization. What do you see, hear, feel, and even smell in this scenario? The more vivid the visualization, the more powerful it becomes.

5. Seek Support:

CAREER GROWTH CAN BE challenging, especially if you're working to overcome self-doubt or navigate a competitive industry. Seek support from mentors, colleagues, or career coaches to help you stay motivated and committed.

Steps for Seeking Support:

1. TALK TO TRUSTED Individuals: Share your career goals and affirmations with trusted mentors or colleagues who can provide encouragement and support.

2. Join Professional Networks: Consider joining professional networks or online communities focused on career growth and development. Sharing experiences and affirmations with others can provide additional motivation and insights.

3. Work with a Career Coach: A career coach can help you create a personalized plan for achieving your career goals and provide guidance on professional development.

Attracting Success and Abundance with Affirmations

SUCCESS AND ABUNDANCE are often the results of a positive mindset, clear goals, and persistent effort. Affirmations can help attract success and abundance by fostering a positive attitude, enhancing your belief in your capabilities, and aligning your actions with your aspirations.

Understanding the Law of Attraction:

THE LAW OF ATTRACTION is based on the idea that like attracts like. Positive thoughts and beliefs can attract positive experiences and outcomes, while negative thoughts can attract negative experiences. Affirmations can help you harness the power of the law of attraction by focusing your mind on success and abundance.

The Role of Affirmations in Attracting Success and Abundance:

AFFIRMATIONS CAN HELP you:

- Develop a success-oriented mindset

- Build confidence in your ability to achieve your goals

- Maintain focus and motivation

- Align your actions with your aspirations

- Attract opportunities and positive outcomes

Steps for Attracting Success and Abundance Through Affirmations:

1. Define Success and Abundance:

BEGIN BY DEFINING WHAT success and abundance mean to you. This could include financial prosperity, career advancement, personal fulfillment, or a combination of factors.

Steps for Defining Success and Abundance:

1. REFLECT ON YOUR Aspirations: Assess your personal and professional aspirations and identify what success and abundance look like for you.

2. Set Specific Goals: Define clear and specific goals related to success and abundance. For example, "I want to achieve financial independence" or "I want to advance to a leadership position."

3. Prioritize Your Goals: Determine which goals are most important to you and focus on creating affirmations for these areas first.

2. Create Success and Abundance Affirmations:

ONCE YOU HAVE DEFINED success and abundance, create affirmations that support these goals. Ensure that these affirmations are positive, specific, and reflect what you want to achieve.

Steps for Creating Success and Abundance Affirmations:

1. REFRAME NEGATIVE Beliefs: Identify any negative beliefs you have about success and abundance and reframe them into positive affirmations. For example, if you believe "I will never be successful," reframe it to "I am capable of achieving great success."

2. Use Positive Language: Use positive language that affirms your ability to attract success and abundance. Avoid using words like "not" or "don't."

3. Be Specific: Make your affirmations specific to your success and abundance goals. For instance, instead of saying "I am successful," say "I am successful in my career and attract abundant opportunities."

Examples of Affirmations for Success and Abundance:

- "I AM OPEN TO RECEIVING abundance in all areas of my life."

- "I attract success and prosperity with my positive mindset and actions."

- "I am worthy of achieving my goals and experiencing abundance."

3. Integrate Affirmations into Your Daily Routine:

CONSISTENCY IS KEY to making affirmations effective. Integrate your success and abundance affirmations into your daily routine to reinforce positive beliefs about your ability to achieve your goals.

Steps for Integrating Affirmations into Your Daily Routine:

1. MORNING RITUAL: Start your day with success and abundance affirmations to set a positive tone. Repeat them while getting ready, during your morning commute, or as part of your morning meditation.

2. Throughout the Day: Use reminders, such as sticky notes or phone alarms, to practice your affirmations throughout the day. Take short breaks to repeat your affirmations and refocus your mind.

3. Evening Reflection: End your day with affirmations to reinforce positive beliefs before sleep. Reflect on your success and abundance goals and use affirmations to acknowledge your progress.

4. Visualize Success and Abundance:

VISUALIZATION CAN ENHANCE the impact of your affirmations. Imagine yourself achieving your success and abundance goals and embodying the qualities you affirm. This helps to create a vivid mental image of prosperity and reinforces your positive beliefs.

Steps for Visualizing Success and Abundance:

1. FIND A QUIET SPACE: Find a quiet and comfortable space where you can relax and focus on your visualization.

2. Close Your Eyes: Close your eyes and take a few deep breaths to center yourself.

3. Visualize Your Affirmations: Visualize yourself living out your success and abundance affirmations. See yourself as successful, prosperous, and fulfilled. Imagine how it feels to achieve your goals and experience abundance.

4. Engage Your Senses: Engage your senses in the visualization. What do you see, hear, feel, and even smell in this scenario? The more vivid the visualization, the more powerful it becomes.

5. Practice Gratitude:

GRATITUDE IS A POWERFUL practice that can enhance your ability to attract success and abundance. By focusing on what you are grateful for, you create a positive mindset that attracts more positive experiences.

Steps for Practicing Gratitude with Affirmations:

1. GRATITUDE JOURNAL: Keep a gratitude journal where you write down three things you are grateful for each day. Reflect on these positive aspects of your life.

2. Gratitude Affirmations: Create affirmations that express gratitude for the success and abundance you already have. For example, "I am grateful for the abundance in my life and the opportunities that come my way."

3. Express Gratitude: Take time each day to express gratitude for your achievements, relationships, and experiences. This practice can enhance your overall well-being and attract more success and abundance.

Examples of Gratitude Affirmations:

- "I AM GRATEFUL FOR the success and abundance in my life."

- "I appreciate the opportunities that come my way and make the most of them."

- "I am thankful for the prosperity and fulfillment I experience."

Real-Life Examples of Career Transformations Through Affirmations

PERSONAL STORIES OF career transformation can provide powerful inspiration and motivation. Here are a few real-life examples of individuals who have used affirmations to achieve significant career success and abundance.

1. Sarah's Journey to Leadership:

SARAH WORKED IN A MID-level management position but always aspired to advance to a leadership role. However, she struggled with self-doubt and lacked confidence in her ability to lead. Determined to overcome these challenges, Sarah decided to use affirmations to build her confidence and achieve her career goals.

Sarah's Affirmation Practice:

SARAH CREATED AFFIRMATIONS that focused on her leadership skills and qualities, such as "I am a confident and effective leader," "I am capable of inspiring and guiding my team," and "I trust in my ability to make sound decisions."

Steps Sarah Took:

1. DAILY PRACTICE: Sarah integrated her affirmations into her daily routine. She repeated them every morning and evening, as well as during moments of self-doubt.

2. Visualization: Sarah visualized herself in a leadership role, confidently leading her team and making impactful decisions.

3. Professional Development: Sarah sought opportunities for professional development, such as leadership training and mentorship programs, to enhance her skills.

4. Seeking Support: Sarah shared her affirmations and goals with trusted mentors and colleagues who provided encouragement and support.

Sarah's Transformation:

OVER TIME, SARAH NOTICED significant changes in her confidence and leadership abilities. She began to take on more responsibilities, actively participated in decision-making processes, and sought out leadership opportunities. Sarah's transformation culminated in her promotion to a senior leadership position, demonstrating the effectiveness of affirmations in achieving career success.

2. Mark's Path to Financial Independence:

MARK WORKED IN A CORPORATE job but always dreamed of achieving financial independence through entrepreneurship. However, he struggled with fear and uncertainty about leaving the security of his job. Determined to pursue his dream, Mark decided to use affirmations to build his confidence and attract financial success.

Mark's Affirmation Practice:

MARK CREATED AFFIRMATIONS that focused on his financial goals and entrepreneurial success, such as "I am confident in my ability to create a successful business," "I attract financial abundance and prosperity," and "I am worthy of achieving financial independence."

Steps Mark Took:

1. MORNING RITUAL MARK started his day with financial success affirmations to set a positive tone and boost his motivation.

2. Visualization: Mark visualized himself running a successful business, attracting clients, and achieving financial independence.

3. Business Plan: Mark developed a detailed business plan and set clear financial goals to guide his entrepreneurial journey.

4. Seeking Support: Mark joined entrepreneurial networks and sought mentorship from successful business owners who provided guidance and encouragement.

Mark's Transformation:

THROUGH CONSISTENT affirmation practice and dedicated effort, Mark gained the confidence to leave his corporate job and start his own business. He attracted clients, grew his business, and achieved financial independence. Mark's transformation highlighted the power of affirmations in attracting success and abundance.

3. Emma's Career Advancement:

EMMA WORKED AS A MARKETING specialist but aspired to advance to a management position. She felt stuck in her current role and doubted her ability to progress. Determined to achieve her career goals, Emma decided to use affirmations to build her confidence and attract career opportunities.

Emma's Affirmation Practice:

EMMA CREATED AFFIRMATIONS that focused on her marketing skills and career advancement, such as "I am a skilled and knowledgeable marketing professional," "I am open to new career opportunities and trust in my ability to succeed," and "I am confident in my ability to lead and manage a marketing team."

Steps Emma Took:

1. DAILY PRACTICE: Emma integrated her affirmations into her daily routine. She repeated them every morning and evening, as well as during moments of self-doubt.

2. Visualization: Emma visualized herself in a management role, leading her marketing team and achieving successful campaign outcomes.

3. Professional Development: Emma sought opportunities for professional development, such as marketing certifications and leadership training, to enhance her skills.

4. Networking: Emma expanded her professional network by attending industry events and connecting with marketing professionals who could provide guidance and support.

Emma's Transformation:

THROUGH CONSISTENT affirmation practice and dedicated effort, Emma gained the confidence to pursue career advancement opportunities. She applied for management positions, demonstrated her skills and expertise, and secured a promotion to a marketing manager role. Emma's transformation showcased the effectiveness of affirmations in achieving career growth and success.

4. David's Path to Entrepreneurial Success:

DAVID HAD A PASSION for technology and dreamed of starting his own tech company. However, he struggled with self-doubt and feared the risks associated with entrepreneurship. Determined to pursue his dream, David decided to use affirmations to build his confidence and attract entrepreneurial success.

David's Affirmation Practice:

DAVID CREATED AFFIRMATIONS that focused on his entrepreneurial skills and success, such as "I am confident in my ability to build a successful tech company," "I attract innovative ideas and opportunities," and "I am capable of overcoming challenges and achieving entrepreneurial success."

Steps David Took:

1. MORNING RITUAL: David started his day with entrepreneurial success affirmations to set a positive tone and boost his motivation.

2. Visualization: David visualized himself running a successful tech company, attracting clients, and achieving business growth.

3. Business Plan: David developed a detailed business plan and set clear goals for his tech company.

4. Seeking Support: David joined entrepreneurial networks and sought mentorship from successful tech entrepreneurs who provided guidance and encouragement.

David's Transformation:

THROUGH CONSISTENT affirmation practice and dedicated effort, David gained the confidence to launch his tech company. He attracted clients, developed innovative products, and achieved significant business growth.

David's transformation highlighted the power of affirmations in attracting entrepreneurial success and abundance.

Conclusion

Affirmations are powerful tools for enhancing career growth and professional development, attracting success and abundance, and achieving significant career transformations. By fostering a positive mindset, increasing motivation, and reinforcing your commitment to achieving your career goals, affirmations can help you overcome self-doubt, build confidence, and create a clear vision for your professional future.

In this chapter, we explored how to enhance career growth through affirmations, attract success and abundance, and shared real-life examples of career transformations. These stories demonstrate the profound impact affirmations can have on individuals' professional lives, providing inspiration and motivation for your own journey.

As you continue to integrate affirmations into your daily routine, remember to be patient and consistent. Positive change takes time, but with dedication and perseverance, you can harness the power of affirmations to transform your career and achieve the success and abundance you desire.

In the following chapters, we will explore specific areas where affirmations can make a significant impact, providing you with the tools and inspiration to harness the full potential of positive thinking.

Chapter 8: Affirmations for Relationships

Improving Relationships with Affirmations

Relationships are a fundamental aspect of our lives, impacting our happiness, well-being, and personal growth. Affirmations can be powerful tools to enhance the quality of your relationships, whether with a partner, family member, friend, or colleague. By cultivating a positive mindset and fostering constructive behaviors, affirmations can help you improve communication, build trust, and deepen your connections.

Understanding the Role of Mindset in Relationships:

YOUR THOUGHTS AND BELIEFS significantly influence your interactions and relationships. A positive mindset can foster empathy, patience, and understanding, while a negative mindset can lead to conflict, resentment, and misunderstandings. Affirmations help shift your mindset towards positivity, enabling you to approach relationships with an open heart and constructive attitude.

The Role of Affirmations in Improving Relationships:

AFFIRMATIONS CAN HELP you:

- Enhance communication and understanding

- Build trust and mutual respect

- Foster empathy and compassion

- Address and resolve conflicts

- Strengthen emotional bonds

Steps for Improving Relationships Through Affirmations:

1. Identify Relationship Goals:

BEGIN BY IDENTIFYING your goals for your relationships. These could include improving communication, resolving conflicts, deepening emotional intimacy, or building trust.

Steps for Identifying Relationship Goals:

1. REFLECT ON YOUR Relationships: Assess your current relationships and identify areas where you want to see improvement.

2. Set Specific Goals: Define clear and specific relationship goals. For example, "I want to communicate more effectively with my partner" or "I want to build trust with my colleagues."

3. Prioritize Your Goals: Determine which goals are most important to you and focus on creating affirmations for these areas first.

2. Create Relationship-Focused Affirmations:

ONCE YOU HAVE IDENTIFIED your relationship goals, create affirmations that support these goals. Ensure that these affirmations are positive, specific, and reflect what you want to achieve.

Steps for Creating Relationship-Focused Affirmations:

1. REFRAME NEGATIVE Beliefs: Identify any negative beliefs you have about your relationships and reframe them into positive affirmations. For example, if you believe "I am not good at communicating," reframe it to "I communicate openly and effectively."

2. Use Positive Language: Use positive language that affirms your ability to improve your relationships. Avoid using words like "not" or "don't."

3. Be Specific: Make your affirmations specific to your relationship goals. For instance, instead of saying "I have good relationships," say "I build strong, trusting, and loving relationships."

Examples of Affirmations for Improving Relationships:

- "I COMMUNICATE OPENLY, honestly, and effectively with my partner."

- "I build trust and mutual respect in all my relationships."

- "I am patient, understanding, and empathetic in my interactions."

3. Integrate Affirmations into Your Daily Routine:

CONSISTENCY IS KEY to making affirmations effective. Integrate your relationship-focused affirmations into your daily routine to reinforce positive beliefs about your interactions.

Steps for Integrating Affirmations into Your Daily Routine:

1. MORNING RITUAL: Start your day with relationship-focused affirmations to set a positive tone. Repeat them while getting ready, during your morning commute, or as part of your morning meditation.

2. Throughout the Day: Use reminders, such as sticky notes or phone alarms, to practice your affirmations throughout the day. Take short breaks to repeat your affirmations and refocus your mind.

3. Evening Reflection: End your day with affirmations to reinforce positive beliefs before sleep. Reflect on your relationship goals and use affirmations to acknowledge your progress.

4. Visualize Positive Interactions:

VISUALIZATION CAN ENHANCE the impact of your affirmations. Imagine yourself engaging in positive interactions and embodying the qualities you affirm. This helps to create a vivid mental image of healthy relationships and reinforces your positive beliefs.

Steps for Visualizing Positive Interactions:

1. FIND A QUIET SPACE: Find a quiet and comfortable space where you can relax and focus on your visualization.

2. Close Your Eyes: Close your eyes and take a few deep breaths to center yourself.

3. Visualize Your Affirmations: Visualize yourself living out your relationship-focused affirmations. See yourself communicating effectively, building trust, and fostering emotional intimacy. Imagine how it feels to achieve your relationship goals and embody these qualities.

4. Engage Your Senses: Engage your senses in the visualization. What do you see, hear, feel, and even smell in this scenario? The more vivid the visualization, the more powerful it becomes.

5. Seek Support:

IMPROVING RELATIONSHIPS can be challenging, especially if you're working to overcome ingrained habits or past hurts. Seek support from friends, family, or a therapist to help you stay motivated and committed.

Steps for Seeking Support:

1. TALK TO TRUSTED Individuals: Share your relationship goals and affirmations with trusted friends or family members who can provide encouragement and support.

2. Join Support Groups: Consider joining support groups or online communities focused on relationship improvement. Sharing experiences and affirmations with others can provide additional motivation and insights.

3. Work with a Therapist: A therapist can help you explore and address underlying issues that impact your relationships. They can also provide guidance on creating and practicing affirmations.

Building Stronger Connections and Fostering Love

AFFIRMATIONS CAN HELP build stronger connections and foster love in your relationships by promoting positive behaviors, enhancing emotional intimacy, and reinforcing your commitment to nurturing your connections.

Understanding the Importance of Emotional Intimacy:

EMOTIONAL INTIMACY is the closeness and connection you feel with another person. It involves sharing your thoughts, feelings, and experiences openly and honestly. Emotional intimacy is crucial for building strong, loving relationships.

The Role of Affirmations in Building Stronger Connections and Fostering Love:

AFFIRMATIONS CAN HELP you:

- Enhance emotional intimacy and connection

- Foster empathy and compassion

- Build trust and mutual respect

- Reinforce your commitment to nurturing your relationships

Steps for Building Stronger Connections and Fostering Love Through Affirmations:

1. Identify Connection Goals:

BEGIN BY IDENTIFYING your goals for building stronger connections and fostering love. These could include enhancing emotional intimacy, increasing empathy, or deepening your commitment to your relationships.

Steps for Identifying Connection Goals:

1. REFLECT ON YOUR Relationships: Assess your current relationships and identify areas where you want to see deeper connections and more love.

2. Set Specific Goals: Define clear and specific connection goals. For example, "I want to deepen emotional intimacy with my partner" or "I want to build a more empathetic relationship with my friend."

3. Prioritize Your Goals: Determine which goals are most important to you and focus on creating affirmations for these areas first.

2. Create Connection-Focused Affirmations:

ONCE YOU HAVE IDENTIFIED your connection goals, create affirmations that support these goals. Ensure that these affirmations are positive, specific, and reflect what you want to achieve.

Steps for Creating Connection-Focused Affirmations:

1. REFRAME NEGATIVE Beliefs: Identify any negative beliefs you have about your ability to connect with others and reframe them into positive affirmations. For example, if you believe "I am not good at expressing my feelings," reframe it to "I express my feelings openly and honestly."

2. Use Positive Language: Use positive language that affirms your ability to build strong connections and foster love. Avoid using words like "not" or "don't."

3. Be Specific: Make your affirmations specific to your connection goals. For instance, instead of saying "I have strong connections," say "I build deep, loving, and emotionally intimate connections."

Examples of Affirmations for Building Stronger Connections:

- "I EXPRESS MY FEELINGS openly, honestly, and with compassion."

- "I am empathetic and understanding in my interactions."

- "I build deep, loving, and emotionally intimate connections."

3. Integrate Affirmations into Your Daily Routine:

CONSISTENCY IS KEY to making affirmations effective. Integrate your connection-focused affirmations into your daily routine to reinforce positive beliefs about your ability to build strong connections.

Steps for Integrating Affirmations into Your Daily Routine:

1. MORNING RITUAL: Start your day with connection-focused affirmations to set a positive tone. Repeat them while getting ready, during your morning commute, or as part of your morning meditation.

2. Throughout the Day: Use reminders, such as sticky notes or phone alarms, to practice your affirmations throughout the day. Take short breaks to repeat your affirmations and refocus your mind.

3. Evening Reflection: End your day with affirmations to reinforce positive beliefs before sleep. Reflect on your connection goals and use affirmations to acknowledge your progress.

4. Visualize Emotional Intimacy:

VISUALIZATION CAN ENHANCE the impact of your affirmations. Imagine yourself engaging in emotionally intimate interactions and embodying the qualities you affirm. This helps to create a vivid mental image of deep connections and reinforces your positive beliefs.

Steps for Visualizing Emotional Intimacy:

1. FIND A QUIET SPACE: Find a quiet and comfortable space where you can relax and focus on your visualization.

2. Close Your Eyes: Close your eyes and take a few deep breaths to center yourself.

3. Visualize Your Affirmations: Visualize yourself living out your connection-focused affirmations. See yourself expressing your feelings openly, building empathy, and deepening emotional intimacy. Imagine how it feels to achieve your connection goals and embody these qualities.

4. Engage Your Senses: Engage your senses in the visualization. What do you see, hear, feel, and even smell in this scenario? The more vivid the visualization, the more powerful it becomes.

5. Practice Active Listening:

ACTIVE LISTENING IS a crucial skill for building stronger connections and fostering love. It involves fully focusing on the speaker, understanding their message, and responding thoughtfully.

Steps for Practicing Active Listening with Affirmations:

1. BE PRESENT: PRACTICE being fully present in your interactions. Focus on the speaker and avoid distractions.

2. Show Empathy: Use affirmations to cultivate empathy and understanding. For example, "I am empathetic and understanding in my interactions."

3. Reflect and Respond: Reflect on what the speaker has said and respond thoughtfully. Use affirmations to reinforce positive communication, such as "I communicate openly, honestly, and effectively."

Examples of Affirmations for Active Listening:

- "I AM PRESENT AND attentive in my interactions."

- "I listen with empathy and understanding."

- "I communicate openly, honestly, and effectively."

Healing from Past Relationship Wounds Through Positive Affirmations

HEALING FROM PAST RELATIONSHIP wounds is essential for building healthy, fulfilling relationships. Affirmations can help you let go of past hurts, cultivate self-compassion, and open your heart to new connections.

Understanding the Impact of Past Relationship Wounds:

PAST RELATIONSHIP WOUNDS, such as betrayal, loss, or unresolved conflicts, can impact your ability to trust and connect with others. Healing these wounds is crucial for moving forward and building healthy relationships.

The Role of Affirmations in Healing Past Relationship Wounds:

AFFIRMATIONS CAN HELP you:

- Let go of past hurts and negative beliefs

- Cultivate self-compassion and forgiveness

- Build trust and openness in new relationships

- Reinforce your commitment to personal growth and healing

Steps for Healing from Past Relationship Wounds Through Affirmations:

1. Identify Relationship Wounds:

BEGIN BY IDENTIFYING the past relationship wounds that need healing. These could include experiences of betrayal, loss, abandonment, or unresolved conflicts.

Steps for Identifying Relationship Wounds:

1. REFLECT ON PAST Relationships: Assess your past relationships and identify experiences that have caused emotional pain or trauma.

2. Acknowledge Your Feelings: Allow yourself to acknowledge and validate your feelings about these experiences. Write down your thoughts and emotions to bring them to your conscious awareness.

3. Set Healing Goals: Define clear and specific goals for healing from past relationship wounds. For example, "I want to let go of resentment and cultivate forgiveness" or "I want to build trust in my new relationships."

2. Create Healing-Focused Affirmations:

ONCE YOU HAVE IDENTIFIED your relationship wounds and healing goals, create affirmations that support your healing journey. Ensure that these affirmations are positive, specific, and reflect what you want to achieve.

Steps for Creating Healing-Focused Affirmations:

1. REFRAME NEGATIVE Beliefs: Identify any negative beliefs you have about your past relationships and reframe them into positive affirmations. For example, if you believe "I will never trust again," reframe it to "I am open to building trust in my relationships."

2. Use Positive Language: Use positive language that affirms your ability to heal and move forward. Avoid using words like "not" or "don't."

3. Be Specific: Make your affirmations specific to your healing goals. For instance, instead of saying "I am healed," say "I release past hurts and open my heart to new connections."

Examples of Affirmations for Healing Past Relationship Wounds:

- "I RELEASE PAST HURTS and embrace healing and forgiveness."

- "I am open to building trust and deepening connections in my relationships."

- "I cultivate self-compassion and understand that healing takes time."

3. Integrate Affirmations into Your Daily Routine:

CONSISTENCY IS KEY to making affirmations effective. Integrate your healing-focused affirmations into your daily routine to reinforce positive beliefs about your ability to heal and move forward.

Steps for Integrating Affirmations into Your Daily Routine:

1. MORNING RITUAL: Start your day with healing-focused affirmations to set a positive tone. Repeat them while getting ready, during your morning commute, or as part of your morning meditation.

2. Throughout the Day: Use reminders, such as sticky notes or phone alarms, to practice your affirmations throughout the day. Take short breaks to repeat your affirmations and refocus your mind.

3. Evening Reflection: End your day with affirmations to reinforce positive beliefs before sleep. Reflect on your healing goals and use affirmations to acknowledge your progress.

4. Visualize Healing and Forgiveness:

VISUALIZATION CAN ENHANCE the impact of your affirmations. Imagine yourself healing from past wounds, cultivating forgiveness, and opening your heart to new connections. This helps to create a vivid mental image of healing and reinforces your positive beliefs.

Steps for Visualizing Healing and Forgiveness:

1. FIND A QUIET SPACE: Find a quiet and comfortable space where you can relax and focus on your visualization.

2. Close Your Eyes: Close your eyes and take a few deep breaths to center yourself.

3. Visualize Your Affirmations: Visualize yourself living out your healing-focused affirmations. See yourself releasing past hurts, embracing forgiveness, and building trust in new relationships. Imagine how it feels to achieve your healing goals and embody these qualities.

4. Engage Your Senses: Engage your senses in the visualization. What do you see, hear, feel, and even smell in this scenario? The more vivid the visualization, the more powerful it becomes.

5. Practice Self-Compassion:

SELF-COMPASSION IS essential for healing from past relationship wounds. It involves treating yourself with the same kindness and understanding that you would offer to a friend.

Steps for Practicing Self-Compassion with Affirmations:

1. ACKNOWLEDGE YOUR Feelings: Recognize and validate your feelings without judgment. Understand that healing is a process and it's okay to feel vulnerable.

2. Use Compassionate Affirmations: Create affirmations that promote self-compassion and understanding. For example, "I am kind and gentle with myself as I heal" or "I forgive myself for any mistakes and embrace growth."

3. Practice Regularly: Integrate self-compassionate affirmations into your daily routine. Use them during moments of self-doubt or when you catch yourself engaging in negative self-talk.

Examples of Self-Compassionate Affirmations:

- "I AM KIND AND GENTLE with myself as I heal and grow."

- "I forgive myself for any mistakes and learn from them."

- "I am worthy of love and respect, and I honor my healing journey."

6. Seek Professional Help:

HEALING FROM PAST RELATIONSHIP wounds can be complex and may require professional support. A therapist can help you explore and address underlying issues, providing guidance and tools for healing.

Steps for Seeking Professional Help:

1. FIND A THERAPIST: Look for a therapist who specializes in relationship issues and emotional healing. Seek recommendations from trusted sources or use online directories.

2. Commit to the Process: Commit to regular therapy sessions and be open to exploring your feelings and experiences. Use affirmations to support your healing journey, such as "I am open to healing and growth through therapy."

3. Integrate Therapy with Affirmations: Combine the insights and tools you gain in therapy with your affirmation practice. Use affirmations to reinforce positive beliefs and behaviors learned in therapy.

Examples of Affirmations for Therapy Support:

- "I AM OPEN TO HEALING and growth through therapy."

- "I trust my therapist and the healing process."

- "I am committed to my healing journey and embrace the support I receive."

Conclusion

Affirmations are powerful tools for improving relationships, building stronger connections, fostering love, and healing from past relationship wounds. By cultivating a positive mindset and fostering constructive behaviors, affirmations can help you enhance communication, build trust, and deepen your emotional bonds.

In this chapter, we explored how to improve relationships through affirmations, build stronger connections and foster love, and heal from past relationship wounds. By integrating affirmations into your daily routine, creating specific and positive affirmations, and combining them with visualization, active listening, self-compassion, and professional support, you can cultivate healthier and more fulfilling relationships.

As you continue to practice affirmations for relationships, remember to be patient and consistent. Positive change takes time, but with dedication and perseverance, you can harness the power of affirmations to transform your relationships and create a life filled with love, connection, and emotional intimacy.

In the following chapters, we will explore specific areas where affirmations can make a significant impact, providing you with the tools and inspiration to harness the full potential of positive thinking.

Chapter 9: Affirmations for Financial Abundance

Shifting Your Mindset Towards Financial Prosperity

Achieving financial abundance begins with cultivating a positive mindset towards money and prosperity. The way you think and feel about money significantly influences your financial outcomes. Affirmations are powerful tools that can help you shift your mindset towards financial prosperity, overcome limiting beliefs, and attract wealth.

Understanding the Role of Mindset in Financial Prosperity:

YOUR MINDSET SHAPES your attitudes, beliefs, and behaviors towards money. A positive financial mindset fosters confidence, proactive behaviors, and an openness to opportunities, while a negative mindset can lead to self-sabotage, fear, and missed opportunities. Affirmations help reprogram your subconscious mind to adopt a wealth-oriented perspective, enabling you to take actions that lead to financial success.

The Role of Affirmations in Shifting Your Financial Mindset:

Affirmations can help you:

- Develop a positive relationship with money

- Overcome limiting beliefs about wealth

- Cultivate a mindset of abundance and prosperity

- Increase financial confidence and resilience

- Attract financial opportunities and success

Steps for Shifting Your Mindset Towards Financial Prosperity Through Affirmations:

1. Identify Limiting Beliefs:

BEGIN BY IDENTIFYING any limiting beliefs you have about money and financial success. These beliefs often stem from past experiences, cultural conditioning, or societal messages.

Steps for Identifying Limiting Beliefs:

1. REFLECT ON YOUR Financial History: Assess your financial history and identify any recurring patterns or negative experiences related to money.

2. Recognize Negative Thoughts: Pay attention to any negative thoughts or feelings you have about money, such as "Money is hard to come by" or "I will never be wealthy."

3. Write Them Down: Write down these limiting beliefs to bring them to your conscious awareness.

2. Reframe Limiting Beliefs into Positive Affirmations:

ONCE YOU HAVE IDENTIFIED your limiting beliefs, reframe them into positive affirmations that reflect a mindset of abundance and prosperity.

Steps for Reframing Limiting Beliefs:

1. IDENTIFY THE OPPOSITE Belief: For each limiting belief, identify the positive opposite. For example, if you believe "Money is hard to come by," the opposite belief could be "Money flows to me easily and effortlessly."

2. Use Positive Language: Ensure that your affirmations are stated in positive language. Avoid using words like "not" or "don't."

3. Be Specific: Make your affirmations specific to your financial goals and desires. For instance, instead of saying "I am wealthy," say "I attract financial abundance and prosperity into my life."

Examples of Affirmations for Shifting Your Financial Mindset:

- "I am worthy of financial abundance and success."

- "Money flows to me easily and effortlessly."

- "I attract wealth and financial opportunities with my positive mindset."

3. Integrate Affirmations into Your Daily Routine:

Consistency is key to making affirmations effective. Integrate your financial abundance affirmations into your daily routine to reinforce positive beliefs about money.

Steps for Integrating Affirmations into Your Daily Routine:

1. MORNING RITUAL: Start your day with financial abundance affirmations to set a positive tone. Repeat them while getting ready, during your morning commute, or as part of your morning meditation.

2. Throughout the Day: Use reminders, such as sticky notes or phone alarms, to practice your affirmations throughout the day. Take short breaks to repeat your affirmations and refocus your mind.

3. Evening Reflection: End your day with affirmations to reinforce positive beliefs before sleep. Reflect on your financial goals and use affirmations to acknowledge your progress.

4. Visualize Financial Prosperity:

VISUALIZATION CAN ENHANCE the impact of your affirmations. Imagine yourself achieving financial prosperity and embodying the qualities you affirm. This helps to create a vivid mental image of wealth and reinforces your positive beliefs.

Steps for Visualizing Financial Prosperity:

1. FIND A QUIET SPACE: Find a quiet and comfortable space where you can relax and focus on your visualization.

2. Close Your Eyes: Close your eyes and take a few deep breaths to center yourself.

3. Visualize Your Affirmations: Visualize yourself living out your financial abundance affirmations. See yourself as financially prosperous, secure, and successful. Imagine how it feels to achieve your financial goals and embody these qualities.

4. Engage Your Senses: Engage your senses in the visualization. What do you see, hear, feel, and even smell in this scenario? The more vivid the visualization, the more powerful it becomes.

5. Seek Financial Education:

KNOWLEDGE IS A KEY component of financial success. Seek financial education to enhance your understanding of money management, investing, and wealth-building strategies.

Steps for Seeking Financial Education:

1. READ FINANCIAL BOOKS: Read books on personal finance, investing, and wealth-building to expand your knowledge. Use affirmations to reinforce your commitment to financial education, such as "I am committed to learning and growing my financial knowledge."

2. Attend Workshops and Seminars: Attend financial workshops, seminars, or online courses to gain practical insights and strategies. Use affirmations to stay motivated, such as "I am open to new financial opportunities and learning."

3. Consult Financial Experts: Seek advice from financial advisors or experts to guide you in making informed financial decisions. Use affirmations to build

confidence in your ability to manage your finances, such as "I trust my financial decisions and take action towards financial success."

Affirmations to Attract Wealth and Financial Security

ATTRACTING WEALTH AND financial security involves cultivating a mindset of abundance and taking consistent actions towards financial goals. Affirmations can help you align your thoughts, beliefs, and actions with your financial aspirations, attracting wealth and creating a sense of financial security.

Understanding the Law of Attraction:

THE LAW OF ATTRACTION is based on the idea that like attracts like. Positive thoughts and beliefs can attract positive experiences and outcomes, while negative thoughts can attract negative experiences. Affirmations help you harness the power of the law of attraction by focusing your mind on wealth and financial security.

The Role of Affirmations in Attracting Wealth and Financial Security:

AFFIRMATIONS CAN HELP you:

- Develop a wealth-oriented mindset

- Increase financial confidence and resilience

- Attract financial opportunities and success

- Maintain focus and motivation towards financial goals

- Reinforce your commitment to financial security

Steps for Attracting Wealth and Financial Security Through Affirmations:

1. Define Wealth and Financial Security:

BEGIN BY DEFINING WHAT wealth and financial security mean to you. This could include financial independence, a certain level of savings, or the ability to support your desired lifestyle.

Steps for Defining Wealth and Financial Security:

1. Reflect on Your Financial Aspirations: Assess your financial aspirations and identify what wealth and financial security look like for you.

2. Set Specific Goals: Define clear and specific financial goals. For example, "I want to achieve financial independence by age 50" or "I want to have six months' worth of savings for financial security."

3. Prioritize Your Goals: Determine which goals are most important to you and focus on creating affirmations for these areas first.

2. Create Wealth and Financial Security Affirmations:

Once you have defined wealth and financial security, create affirmations that support these goals. Ensure that these affirmations are positive, specific, and reflect what you want to achieve.

Steps for Creating Wealth and Financial Security Affirmations:

1. REFRAME NEGATIVE Beliefs: Identify any negative beliefs you have about wealth and financial security and reframe them into positive affirmations. For example, if you believe "I will never be financially secure," reframe it to "I am creating financial security and abundance in my life."

2. Use Positive Language: Use positive language that affirms your ability to attract wealth and financial security. Avoid using words like "not" or "don't."

3. Be Specific: Make your affirmations specific to your financial goals. For instance, instead of saying "I am wealthy," say "I attract wealth and financial opportunities with my positive mindset and actions."

Examples of Affirmations for Attracting Wealth and Financial Security:

- "I AM OPEN TO RECEIVING wealth and financial abundance in all areas of my life."

- "I attract financial opportunities and success with my positive mindset and actions."

- "I am financially secure and confident in my ability to manage my finances."

3. Integrate Affirmations into Your Daily Routine:

CONSISTENCY IS KEY to making affirmations effective. Integrate your wealth and financial security affirmations into your daily routine to reinforce positive beliefs about money.

Steps for Integrating Affirmations into Your Daily Routine:

1. MORNING RITUAL: Start your day with wealth and financial security affirmations to set a positive tone. Repeat them while getting ready, during your morning commute, or as part of your morning meditation.

2. Throughout the Day: Use reminders, such as sticky notes or phone alarms, to practice your affirmations throughout the day. Take short breaks to repeat your affirmations and refocus your mind.

3. Evening Reflection: End your day with affirmations to reinforce positive beliefs before sleep. Reflect on your financial goals and use affirmations to acknowledge your progress.

4. Visualize Financial Abundance:

VISUALIZATION CAN ENHANCE the impact of your affirmations. Imagine yourself achieving financial abundance and embodying the qualities you affirm. This helps to create a vivid mental image of wealth and reinforces your positive beliefs.

Steps for Visualizing Financial Abundance:

1. FIND A QUIET SPACE: Find a quiet and comfortable space where you can relax and focus on your visualization.

2. Close Your Eyes: Close your eyes and take a few deep breaths to center yourself.

3. Visualize Your Affirmations: Visualize yourself living out your wealth and financial security affirmations. See yourself as financially prosperous, secure, and successful. Imagine how it feels to achieve your financial goals and embody these qualities.

4. Engage Your Senses: Engage your senses in the visualization. What do you see, hear, feel, and even smell in this scenario? The more vivid the visualization, the more powerful it becomes.

5. Take Inspired Action:

AFFIRMATIONS ARE MOST effective when combined with inspired action. Take consistent actions towards your financial goals, guided by your affirmations and positive mindset.

Steps for Taking Inspired Action:

1. SET CLEAR ACTION Steps: Break down your financial goals into clear and actionable steps. For example, if your goal is to save a certain amount, outline the steps you need to take to achieve this, such as setting a budget and reducing expenses.

2. Stay Committed: Use affirmations to stay committed to your action steps. For example, "I am disciplined and committed to achieving my financial goals."

3. Celebrate Progress: Acknowledge and celebrate your progress along the way. Use affirmations to reinforce your achievements, such as "I am proud of my financial progress and continue to move forward with confidence."

Examples of Affirmations for Taking Inspired Action:

- "I AM DISCIPLINED and committed to achieving my financial goals."

- "I take inspired actions towards wealth and financial abundance."

- "I celebrate my financial progress and continue to move forward with confidence."

Stories of Financial Success Through the Power of Affirmations

PERSONAL STORIES OF financial success can provide powerful inspiration and motivation. Here are a few real-life examples of individuals who have used affirmations to achieve significant financial success and abundance.

1. Emily's Journey to Financial Independence:

EMILY WORKED IN A CORPORATE job but always dreamed of achieving financial independence and retiring early. However, she struggled with fear and uncertainty about her financial future. Determined to achieve her goal, Emily decided to use affirmations to build her confidence and attract financial success.

Emily's Affirmation Practice:

EMILY CREATED AFFIRMATIONS that focused on her financial independence and abundance, such as "I am confident in my ability to achieve financial independence," "I attract wealth and financial opportunities with my positive mindset," and "I am financially secure and confident in my future."

Steps Emily Took:

1. DAILY PRACTICE: Emily integrated her affirmations into her daily routine. She repeated them every morning and evening, as well as during moments of self-doubt.

2. Visualization: Emily visualized herself achieving financial independence, enjoying her retirement, and living a financially abundant life.

3. Financial Planning: Emily developed a detailed financial plan, including saving, investing, and budgeting strategies to achieve her goal.

4. Seeking Support: Emily sought advice from financial advisors and joined financial independence communities for guidance and encouragement.

Emily's Transformation:

THROUGH CONSISTENT affirmation practice and dedicated effort, Emily gained the confidence to take control of her finances. She implemented her financial plan, made wise investments, and achieved financial independence earlier than she had initially planned. Emily's transformation highlighted the power of affirmations in attracting financial success and abundance.

2. Michael's Path to Entrepreneurial Success:

MICHAEL HAD A PASSION for entrepreneurship and dreamed of starting his own business. However, he struggled with self-doubt and feared the risks associated with entrepreneurship. Determined to pursue his dream, Michael decided to use affirmations to build his confidence and attract business success.

Michael's Affirmation Practice:

MICHAEL CREATED AFFIRMATIONS that focused on his entrepreneurial success and financial abundance, such as "I am confident in my ability to build a successful business," "I attract financial opportunities and wealth with my positive mindset," and "I am open to receiving abundance in my business."

Steps Michael Took:

1. MORNING RITUAL: Michael started his day with entrepreneurial success affirmations to set a positive tone and boost his motivation.

2. Visualization: Michael visualized himself running a successful business, attracting clients, and achieving financial abundance.

3. Business Plan: Michael developed a detailed business plan and set clear goals for his business.

4. Seeking Support: Michael joined entrepreneurial networks and sought mentorship from successful business owners who provided guidance and encouragement.

Michael's Transformation:

THROUGH CONSISTENT affirmation practice and dedicated effort, Michael gained the confidence to launch his business. He attracted clients, grew his business, and achieved significant financial success. Michael's transformation highlighted the power of affirmations in attracting entrepreneurial success and financial abundance.

3. Sarah's Financial Turnaround:

SARAH HAD ALWAYS STRUGGLED with managing her finances and was burdened with debt. She felt overwhelmed and believed she would never achieve financial security. Determined to turn her financial situation around, Sarah decided to use affirmations to build her confidence and attract financial stability.

Sarah's Affirmation Practice:

SARAH CREATED AFFIRMATIONS that focused on financial security and abundance, such as "I am confident in my ability to manage my finances," "I attract wealth and financial stability with my positive mindset," and "I am debt-free and financially secure."

Steps Sarah Took:

1. DAILY PRACTICE: Sarah integrated her affirmations into her daily routine. She repeated them every morning and evening, as well as during moments of financial stress.

2. Visualization: Sarah visualized herself debt-free, financially secure, and living a life of financial abundance.

3. Debt Repayment Plan: Sarah developed a detailed debt repayment plan, including budgeting and saving strategies to achieve her goal.

4. Seeking Support: Sarah sought advice from financial advisors and joined financial support groups for guidance and encouragement.

Sarah's Transformation:

THROUGH CONSISTENT affirmation practice and dedicated effort, Sarah gained the confidence to take control of her finances. She implemented her debt repayment plan, reduced her expenses, and eventually became debt-free. Sarah's transformation highlighted the power of affirmations in achieving financial stability and abundance.

4. David's Wealth-Building Journey:

DAVID HAD A STABLE job but always aspired to build significant wealth and achieve financial freedom. However, he struggled with limiting beliefs about his ability to accumulate wealth. Determined to change his financial future, David decided to use affirmations to build his confidence and attract wealth.

David's Affirmation Practice:

DAVID CREATED AFFIRMATIONS that focused on wealth-building and financial abundance, such as "I am confident in my ability to build wealth," "I attract financial opportunities and abundance with my positive mindset," and "I am financially free and live a life of prosperity."

Steps David Took:

1. MORNING RITUAL: David started his day with wealth-building affirmations to set a positive tone and boost his motivation.

2. Visualization: David visualized himself building wealth, making successful investments, and living a life of financial freedom.

3. Investment Plan: David developed a detailed investment plan, including stocks, real estate, and other wealth-building strategies.

4. Seeking Support: David sought advice from financial advisors and joined investment communities for guidance and encouragement.

David's Transformation:

THROUGH CONSISTENT affirmation practice and dedicated effort, David gained the confidence to take control of his wealth-building journey. He made strategic investments, grew his wealth, and achieved financial freedom. David's transformation highlighted the power of affirmations in attracting wealth and financial abundance.

Conclusion

Affirmations are powerful tools for shifting your mindset towards financial prosperity, attracting wealth and financial security, and achieving significant financial success. By cultivating a positive mindset, increasing financial confidence, and reinforcing your commitment to financial goals, affirmations can help you overcome limiting beliefs, attract financial opportunities, and create a life of abundance.

In this chapter, we explored how to shift your mindset towards financial prosperity through affirmations, attract wealth and financial security, and shared real-life examples of financial success through the power of affirmations. These stories demonstrate the profound impact affirmations can have on individuals' financial lives, providing inspiration and motivation for your own journey.

As you continue to practice affirmations for financial abundance, remember to be patient and consistent. Positive change takes time, but with dedication and perseverance, you can harness the power of affirmations to transform your financial situation and achieve the wealth and financial security you desire.

In the following chapters, we will explore specific areas where affirmations can make a significant impact, providing you with the tools and inspiration to harness the full potential of positive thinking.

Chapter 10: Affirmations for Personal Growth and Development

Setting Personal Goals and Achieving Them with Affirmations

Personal growth and development are lifelong pursuits that enable you to reach your full potential, enhance your well-being, and achieve a fulfilling life. Affirmations can be powerful tools to help you set personal goals, stay motivated, and achieve your aspirations. By regularly practicing affirmations, you can cultivate a positive mindset, overcome self-doubt, and reinforce your commitment to personal growth.

Understanding the Importance of Personal Goals:

PERSONAL GOALS GIVE direction and purpose to your life. They help you focus your efforts, measure your progress, and stay motivated. Setting and achieving personal goals can lead to a sense of accomplishment, increased confidence, and continuous personal growth.

The Role of Affirmations in Setting and Achieving Personal Goals:

AFFIRMATIONS CAN HELP you:

- Clarify and define your personal goals

- Build confidence in your ability to achieve your goals

- Maintain motivation and focus

- Overcome obstacles and setbacks

- Reinforce a growth-oriented mindset

Steps for Setting Personal Goals and Achieving Them with Affirmations:

1. Identify Personal Goals:

BEGIN BY IDENTIFYING your personal goals. These could include areas such as career, health, relationships, personal development, or hobbies.

Steps for Identifying Personal Goals:

1. REFLECT ON YOUR Aspirations: Assess your aspirations and identify what you want to achieve in different areas of your life.

2. Set Specific Goals: Define clear and specific goals. For example, "I want to run a marathon," "I want to learn a new language," or "I want to improve my public speaking skills."

3. Prioritize Your Goals: Determine which goals are most important to you and focus on creating affirmations for these areas first.

2. Create Goal-Focused Affirmations:

ONCE YOU HAVE IDENTIFIED your personal goals, create affirmations that support these goals. Ensure that these affirmations are positive, specific, and reflect what you want to achieve.

Steps for Creating Goal-Focused Affirmations:

1. REFRAME NEGATIVE Beliefs: Identify any negative beliefs you have about your ability to achieve your goals and reframe them into positive affirmations. For example, if you believe "I can't run a marathon," reframe it to "I am capable of running a marathon and achieving my fitness goals."

2. Use Positive Language: Use positive language that affirms your ability to achieve your goals. Avoid using words like "not" or "don't."

3. Be Specific: Make your affirmations specific to your goals. For instance, instead of saying "I am successful," say "I successfully complete my marathon training and achieve my fitness goals."

Examples of Affirmations for Setting and Achieving Personal Goals:

- "I AM CAPABLE OF ACHIEVING my personal goals and aspirations."

- "I stay focused and motivated in pursuing my goals."

- "I overcome any obstacles and achieve my goals with confidence."

3. Integrate Affirmations into Your Daily Routine:

CONSISTENCY IS KEY to making affirmations effective. Integrate your goal-focused affirmations into your daily routine to reinforce positive beliefs about your ability to achieve your goals.

Steps for Integrating Affirmations into Your Daily Routine:

1. MORNING RITUAL: Start your day with goal-focused affirmations to set a positive tone. Repeat them while getting ready, during your morning commute, or as part of your morning meditation.

2. Throughout the Day: Use reminders, such as sticky notes or phone alarms, to practice your affirmations throughout the day. Take short breaks to repeat your affirmations and refocus your mind.

3. Evening Reflection: End your day with affirmations to reinforce positive beliefs before sleep. Reflect on your goals and use affirmations to acknowledge your progress.

4. Visualize Achieving Your Goals:

VISUALIZATION CAN ENHANCE the impact of your affirmations. Imagine yourself achieving your personal goals and embodying the qualities you affirm. This helps to create a vivid mental image of success and reinforces your positive beliefs.

Steps for Visualizing Achieving Your Goals:

1. FIND A QUIET SPACE: Find a quiet and comfortable space where you can relax and focus on your visualization.

2. Close Your Eyes: Close your eyes and take a few deep breaths to center yourself.

3. Visualize Your Affirmations: Visualize yourself living out your goal-focused affirmations. See yourself achieving your personal goals, feeling accomplished, and embodying the qualities you affirm. Imagine how it feels to achieve your goals and embody these qualities.

4. Engage Your Senses: Engage your senses in the visualization. What do you see, hear, feel, and even smell in this scenario? The more vivid the visualization, the more powerful it becomes.

5. Track Your Progress:

TRACKING YOUR PROGRESS is essential for staying motivated and measuring your achievements. Use affirmations to celebrate your progress and reinforce your commitment to your goals.

Steps for Tracking Your Progress:

1. SET MILESTONES: Break down your goals into smaller, manageable milestones. For example, if your goal is to run a marathon, set milestones for different stages of your training.

2. Keep a Journal: Maintain a journal to track your progress and reflect on your achievements. Use affirmations to acknowledge your efforts and celebrate your milestones.

3. Adjust as Needed: Be open to adjusting your goals and action steps based on your progress. Use affirmations to stay flexible and committed, such as "I adapt to challenges and continue to move forward with confidence."

Examples of Affirmations for Tracking Progress:

- "I CELEBRATE MY PROGRESS and acknowledge my achievements."

- "I stay committed to my goals and adjust my approach as needed."

- "I am proud of my efforts and continue to move forward with confidence."

Enhancing Personal Growth and Self-Improvement

PERSONAL GROWTH AND self-improvement are ongoing processes that involve continuously striving to become the best version of yourself. Affirmations can help you cultivate a growth-oriented mindset, overcome self-limiting beliefs, and enhance your commitment to self-improvement.

Understanding the Importance of a Growth Mindset:

A GROWTH MINDSET IS the belief that your abilities and intelligence can be developed through dedication, effort, and continuous learning. This mindset encourages resilience, curiosity, and a willingness to embrace challenges.

The Role of Affirmations in Enhancing Personal Growth and Self-Improvement:

AFFIRMATIONS CAN HELP you:

- Cultivate a growth-oriented mindset

- Overcome self-limiting beliefs

- Foster a love of learning and self-improvement

- Build resilience and perseverance

- Reinforce your commitment to personal growth

Steps for Enhancing Personal Growth and Self-Improvement Through Affirmations:

1. Identify Areas for Growth:

BEGIN BY IDENTIFYING areas where you want to experience personal growth and self-improvement. These could include skills, habits, knowledge, or personal qualities.

Steps for Identifying Areas for Growth:

1. REFLECT ON YOUR Life: Assess different areas of your life and identify where you want to see growth and improvement.

2. Set Specific Goals: Define clear and specific growth goals. For example, "I want to improve my time management skills," "I want to become more resilient," or "I want to develop better communication skills."

3. Prioritize Your Goals: Determine which areas for growth are most important to you and focus on creating affirmations for these areas first.

2. Create Growth-Focused Affirmations:

ONCE YOU HAVE IDENTIFIED your areas for growth, create affirmations that support your self-improvement goals. Ensure that these affirmations are positive, specific, and reflect what you want to achieve.

Steps for Creating Growth-Focused Affirmations:

1. REFRAME NEGATIVE Beliefs: Identify any negative beliefs you have about your ability to grow and improve and reframe them into positive affirmations. For example, if you believe "I can't improve my time management," reframe it to "I am capable of improving my time management skills and becoming more efficient."

2. Use Positive Language: Use positive language that affirms your ability to grow and improve. Avoid using words like "not" or "don't."

3. Be Specific: Make your affirmations specific to your growth goals. For instance, instead of saying "I am improving," say "I consistently improve my time management skills and become more efficient."

Examples of Affirmations for Enhancing Personal Growth:

- "I AM COMMITTED TO continuous learning and self-improvement."

- "I embrace challenges as opportunities for growth and learning."

- "I am resilient and persevere through obstacles with confidence."

3. Integrate Affirmations into Your Daily Routine:

CONSISTENCY IS KEY to making affirmations effective. Integrate your growth-focused affirmations into your daily routine to reinforce positive beliefs about your ability to grow and improve.

Steps for Integrating Affirmations into Your Daily Routine:

1. MORNING RITUAL: Start your day with growth-focused affirmations to set a positive tone. Repeat them while getting ready, during your morning commute, or as part of your morning meditation.

2. Throughout the Day: Use reminders, such as sticky notes or phone alarms, to practice your affirmations throughout the day. Take short breaks to repeat your affirmations and refocus your mind.

3. Evening Reflection: End your day with affirmations to reinforce positive beliefs before sleep. Reflect on your growth goals and use affirmations to acknowledge your progress.

4. Visualize Personal Growth:

VISUALIZATION CAN ENHANCE the impact of your affirmations. Imagine yourself achieving personal growth and embodying the qualities you affirm. This helps to create a vivid mental image of growth and reinforces your positive beliefs.

Steps for Visualizing Personal Growth:

1. FIND A QUIET SPACE: Find a quiet and comfortable space where you can relax and focus on your visualization.

2. Close Your Eyes: Close your eyes and take a few deep breaths to center yourself.

3. Visualize Your Affirmations: Visualize yourself living out your growth-focused affirmations. See yourself learning new skills, embracing challenges, and becoming more resilient. Imagine how it feels to achieve your growth goals and embody these qualities.

4. Engage Your Senses: Engage your senses in the visualization. What do you see, hear, feel, and even smell in this scenario? The more vivid the visualization, the more powerful it becomes.

5. Seek Opportunities for Learning:

CONTINUOUS LEARNING is essential for personal growth and self-improvement. Seek opportunities to expand your knowledge, develop new skills, and gain new experiences.

Steps for Seeking Opportunities for Learning:

1. READ BOOKS: READ books on personal development, self-improvement, and subjects that interest you. Use affirmations to reinforce your love of learning, such as "I am committed to continuous learning and self-improvement."

2. Attend Workshops and Seminars: Attend workshops, seminars, or online courses to gain practical insights and strategies. Use affirmations to stay motivated, such as "I am open to new opportunities for growth and learning."

3. Engage in New Experiences: Seek out new experiences that challenge you and help you grow. Use affirmations to build confidence in your ability to embrace new experiences, such as "I embrace new experiences with confidence and curiosity."

Examples of Affirmations for Continuous Learning:

- "I AM COMMITTED TO continuous learning and self-improvement."

- "I am open to new opportunities for growth and learning."

- "I embrace new experiences with confidence and curiosity."

Techniques for Continuous Personal Development

CONTINUOUS PERSONAL development is a lifelong journey that involves regularly assessing your progress, setting new goals, and seeking opportunities for growth. Affirmations can help you stay committed to your personal development journey, overcome challenges, and celebrate your progress.

Understanding the Importance of Continuous Personal Development:

CONTINUOUS PERSONAL development is essential for achieving your full potential, enhancing your well-being, and leading a fulfilling life. It involves regularly setting and achieving new goals, seeking opportunities for growth, and embracing a mindset of continuous learning.

The Role of Affirmations in Continuous Personal Development:

AFFIRMATIONS CAN HELP you:

- Stay committed to your personal development journey

- Overcome challenges and setbacks

- Maintain motivation and focus

- Celebrate your progress and achievements

- Reinforce a growth-oriented mindset

Steps for Continuous Personal Development Through Affirmations:

1. Regularly Assess Your Progress:

REGULARLY ASSESSING your progress is essential for staying motivated and measuring your achievements. Use affirmations to celebrate your progress and reinforce your commitment to personal development.

Steps for Regularly Assessing Your Progress:

1. SET MILESTONES: Break down your personal development goals into smaller, manageable milestones. For example, if your goal is to improve your public speaking skills, set milestones for different stages of your development.

2. Keep a Journal: Maintain a journal to track your progress and reflect on your achievements. Use affirmations to acknowledge your efforts and celebrate your milestones.

3. Reflect Regularly: Set aside regular times to reflect on your progress and adjust your goals and action steps as needed. Use affirmations to stay flexible and committed, such as "I adapt to challenges and continue to move forward with confidence."

Examples of Affirmations for Regularly Assessing Progress:

- "I CELEBRATE MY PROGRESS and acknowledge my achievements."

- "I stay committed to my personal development and adjust my approach as needed."

- "I am proud of my efforts and continue to move forward with confidence."

2. Set New Goals:

SETTING NEW GOALS IS essential for continuous personal development. Use affirmations to stay motivated and focused on your new goals.

Steps for Setting New Goals:

1. REFLECT ON YOUR Progress: Assess your progress and identify areas where you want to set new goals. Use affirmations to stay motivated, such as "I am committed to continuous learning and self-improvement."

2. Set Specific Goals: Define clear and specific new goals. For example, "I want to learn a new skill," "I want to develop a new habit," or "I want to achieve a new level of fitness."

3. Prioritize Your Goals: Determine which new goals are most important to you and focus on creating affirmations for these areas first.

Examples of Affirmations for Setting New Goals:

- "I AM COMMITTED TO continuous learning and self-improvement."

- "I set new goals and stay motivated to achieve them."

- "I am focused and dedicated to achieving my new goals."

3. Seek Opportunities for Growth:

SEEKING OPPORTUNITIES for growth is essential for continuous personal development. Use affirmations to stay open to new experiences and opportunities.

Steps for Seeking Opportunities for Growth:

1. EXPLORE NEW INTERESTS: Seek out new interests and activities that challenge you and help you grow. Use affirmations to build confidence in your ability to embrace new experiences, such as "I embrace new experiences with confidence and curiosity."

2. Join Groups and Communities: Join groups or communities focused on personal development and self-improvement. Use affirmations to stay motivated, such as "I am open to new opportunities for growth and learning."

3. Seek Mentorship: Seek mentorship from individuals who can guide and support you in your personal development journey. Use affirmations to stay open to receiving guidance, such as "I am open to receiving guidance and support from mentors."

Examples of Affirmations for Seeking Opportunities for Growth:

- "I AM COMMITTED TO continuous learning and self-improvement."

- "I am open to new opportunities for growth and learning."

- "I embrace new experiences with confidence and curiosity."

4. Overcome Challenges and Setbacks:

OVERCOMING CHALLENGES and setbacks is essential for continuous personal development. Use affirmations to build resilience and perseverance.

Steps for Overcoming Challenges and Setbacks:

1. ACKNOWLEDGE YOUR Feelings: Recognize and validate your feelings about challenges and setbacks without judgment. Use affirmations to stay resilient, such as "I am resilient and persevere through obstacles with confidence."

2. Reframe Challenges: Reframe challenges as opportunities for growth and learning. Use affirmations to stay motivated, such as "I embrace challenges as opportunities for growth and learning."

3. Seek Support: Seek support from friends, family, or a mentor to help you navigate challenges and setbacks. Use affirmations to stay open to receiving support, such as "I am open to receiving guidance and support from others."

Examples of Affirmations for Overcoming Challenges:

- "I AM RESILIENT AND persevere through obstacles with confidence."

- "I embrace challenges as opportunities for growth and learning."

- "I seek and receive support from others with gratitude."

5. Celebrate Your Progress and Achievements:

CELEBRATING YOUR PROGRESS and achievements is essential for staying motivated and acknowledging your efforts. Use affirmations to celebrate your achievements and reinforce your commitment to personal development.

Steps for Celebrating Your Progress and Achievements:

1. ACKNOWLEDGE YOUR Efforts: Take time to acknowledge and celebrate your efforts and achievements. Use affirmations to reinforce your achievements, such as "I am proud of my progress and celebrate my achievements."

2. Reward Yourself: Reward yourself for reaching milestones and achieving goals. Use affirmations to stay motivated, such as "I celebrate my progress and acknowledge my achievements."

3. Reflect on Your Journey: Reflect on your personal development journey and the progress you have made. Use affirmations to stay committed to continuous

growth, such as "I am committed to continuous learning and self-improvement."

Examples of Affirmations for Celebrating Achievements:

- "I AM PROUD OF MY progress and celebrate my achievements."

- "I acknowledge my efforts and reward myself for my achievements."

- "I reflect on my journey and stay committed to continuous growth."

Conclusion

Affirmations are powerful tools for setting personal goals, enhancing personal growth and self-improvement, and staying committed to continuous personal development. By cultivating a growth-oriented mindset, overcoming self-limiting beliefs, and reinforcing your commitment to self-improvement, affirmations can help you achieve your full potential and lead a fulfilling life.

In this chapter, we explored how to set personal goals and achieve them with affirmations, enhance personal growth and self-improvement, and use techniques for continuous personal development. By integrating affirmations into your daily routine, creating specific and positive affirmations, and combining them with visualization, tracking progress, seeking opportunities for learning, and celebrating achievements, you can cultivate a mindset of continuous growth and achieve your personal development goals.

As you continue to practice affirmations for personal growth and development, remember to be patient and consistent. Positive change takes time, but with dedication and perseverance, you can harness the power of affirmations to transform your life and achieve your aspirations.

In the following chapters, we will explore specific areas where affirmations can make a significant impact, providing you with the tools and inspiration to harness the full potential of positive thinking.

Chapter 11: Overcoming Obstacles with Affirmations

Using Affirmations to Face and Overcome Challenges

Life is filled with obstacles and challenges that test our strength, resilience, and determination. Whether it's a personal setback, a professional hurdle, or an emotional struggle, these obstacles can sometimes seem insurmountable. However, with the right mindset and tools, you can face and overcome these challenges, emerging stronger and more resilient. Affirmations are powerful tools that can help you cultivate the mindset needed to overcome obstacles and achieve your goals.

Understanding the Role of Mindset in Overcoming Obstacles:

YOUR MINDSET PLAYS a crucial role in how you perceive and respond to challenges. A positive mindset can help you approach obstacles with confidence, determination, and resilience, while a negative mindset can lead to fear, self-doubt, and defeat. Affirmations help shift your mindset towards positivity, enabling you to face and overcome challenges with a proactive and empowered attitude.

The Role of Affirmations in Overcoming Obstacles:

AFFIRMATIONS CAN HELP you:

- Build confidence and self-belief

- Maintain focus and motivation

- Cultivate resilience and perseverance

- Reframe challenges as opportunities for growth

- Reinforce a proactive and empowered mindset

Steps for Using Affirmations to Face and Overcome Challenges:

1. Identify the Obstacles:

BEGIN BY IDENTIFYING the obstacles you are facing. These could be personal, professional, or emotional challenges that are preventing you from achieving your goals.

Steps for Identifying Obstacles:

1. REFLECT ON YOUR Challenges: Assess different areas of your life and identify the challenges and obstacles you are facing.

2. Acknowledge Your Feelings: Allow yourself to acknowledge and validate your feelings about these obstacles. Write down your thoughts and emotions to bring them to your conscious awareness.

3. Set Clear Goals: Define clear and specific goals for overcoming these obstacles. For example, "I want to overcome my fear of public speaking," "I want to improve my time management skills," or "I want to rebuild my confidence after a setback."

2. Create Empowering Affirmations:

ONCE YOU HAVE IDENTIFIED your obstacles, create affirmations that empower you to overcome these challenges. Ensure that these affirmations are positive, specific, and reflect what you want to achieve.

Steps for Creating Empowering Affirmations:

1. REFRAME NEGATIVE Beliefs: Identify any negative beliefs you have about your ability to overcome obstacles and reframe them into positive affirmations. For example, if you believe "I can't handle this challenge," reframe it to "I am capable of overcoming this challenge with confidence."

2. Use Positive Language: Use positive language that affirms your ability to overcome obstacles. Avoid using words like "not" or "don't."

3. Be Specific: Make your affirmations specific to the challenges you are facing. For instance, instead of saying "I am strong," say "I am strong and resilient in the face of challenges."

Examples of Affirmations for Overcoming Obstacles:

- "I AM CAPABLE OF OVERCOMING any challenge that comes my way."

- "I face obstacles with confidence, resilience, and determination."

- "I am proactive and empowered in overcoming challenges."

3. Integrate Affirmations into Your Daily Routine:

Consistency is key to making affirmations effective. Integrate your empowering affirmations into your daily routine to reinforce positive beliefs about your ability to overcome obstacles.

Steps for Integrating Affirmations into Your Daily Routine:

1. MORNING RITUAL: Start your day with affirmations to set a positive tone. Repeat them while getting ready, during your morning commute, or as part of your morning meditation.

2. Throughout the Day: Use reminders, such as sticky notes or phone alarms, to practice your affirmations throughout the day. Take short breaks to repeat your affirmations and refocus your mind.

3. Evening Reflection: End your day with affirmations to reinforce positive beliefs before sleep. Reflect on the challenges you faced during the day and use affirmations to acknowledge your progress and resilience.

4. Visualize Overcoming Challenges:

VISUALIZATION CAN ENHANCE the impact of your affirmations. Imagine yourself successfully overcoming obstacles and embodying the qualities you affirm. This helps to create a vivid mental image of resilience and reinforces your positive beliefs.

Steps for Visualizing Overcoming Challenges:

1. FIND A QUIET SPACE: Find a quiet and comfortable space where you can relax and focus on your visualization.

2. Close Your Eyes: Close your eyes and take a few deep breaths to center yourself.

3. Visualize Your Affirmations: Visualize yourself living out your empowering affirmations. See yourself overcoming obstacles with confidence, resilience, and determination. Imagine how it feels to achieve your goals and embody these qualities.

4. Engage Your Senses: Engage your senses in the visualization. What do you see, hear, feel, and even smell in this scenario? The more vivid the visualization, the more powerful it becomes.

5. Reframe Challenges as Opportunities:

REFRAMING CHALLENGES as opportunities for growth can help you approach obstacles with a positive and proactive mindset. Use affirmations to shift your perspective and embrace challenges as opportunities to learn and grow.

Steps for Reframing Challenges:

1. ACKNOWLEDGE THE Challenge: Recognize and validate the challenge you are facing without judgment.

2. Identify the Opportunity: Identify the potential opportunity for growth and learning within the challenge. Use affirmations to reinforce this perspective, such as "I embrace challenges as opportunities for growth and learning."

3. Stay Positive: Use affirmations to maintain a positive and proactive mindset. For example, "I am resilient and embrace challenges with confidence."

Examples of Affirmations for Reframing Challenges:

- "I EMBRACE CHALLENGES as opportunities for growth and learning."

- "I am resilient and approach challenges with a positive mindset."

- "I learn and grow from every challenge I face."

Building Resilience and Perseverance

RESILIENCE AND PERSEVERANCE are essential qualities for overcoming obstacles and achieving your goals. They enable you to bounce back from setbacks, stay committed to your goals, and maintain a positive attitude in the face of adversity. Affirmations can help you build resilience and perseverance by reinforcing your belief in your ability to overcome challenges and stay motivated.

Understanding the Importance of Resilience and Perseverance:

RESILIENCE IS THE ABILITY to recover from setbacks and adapt to challenging circumstances. Perseverance is the steadfast determination to continue pursuing your goals despite difficulties and obstacles. Together, these qualities enable you to navigate life's challenges with strength and determination.

The Role of Affirmations in Building Resilience and Perseverance:

AFFIRMATIONS CAN HELP you:

- Cultivate a resilient and determined mindset

- Overcome self-doubt and fear

- Maintain motivation and focus

- Reinforce your commitment to your goals

- Build confidence in your ability to persevere

Steps for Building Resilience and Perseverance Through Affirmations:

1. Identify Areas for Growth:

BEGIN BY IDENTIFYING areas where you want to build resilience and perseverance. These could include personal, professional, or emotional challenges.

Steps for Identifying Areas for Growth:

1. REFLECT ON YOUR Challenges: Assess different areas of your life and identify challenges where you want to build resilience and perseverance.

2. Set Specific Goals: Define clear and specific goals for building resilience and perseverance. For example, "I want to become more resilient in handling stress," "I want to persevere through difficult projects," or "I want to maintain a positive attitude in the face of setbacks."

3. Prioritize Your Goals: Determine which areas for growth are most important to you and focus on creating affirmations for these areas first.

2. Create Resilience and Perseverance Affirmations:

ONCE YOU HAVE IDENTIFIED your areas for growth, create affirmations that support your goals for building resilience and perseverance. Ensure that these affirmations are positive, specific, and reflect what you want to achieve.

Steps for Creating Resilience and Perseverance Affirmations:

1. REFRAME NEGATIVE Beliefs: Identify any negative beliefs you have about your ability to be resilient and persevere and reframe them into positive affirmations. For example, if you believe "I can't handle stress," reframe it to "I am resilient and handle stress with confidence."

2. Use Positive Language: Use positive language that affirms your ability to be resilient and persevere. Avoid using words like "not" or "don't."

3. Be Specific: Make your affirmations specific to your goals for resilience and perseverance. For instance, instead of saying "I am resilient," say "I am resilient and persevere through challenges with confidence."

Examples of Affirmations for Building Resilience and Perseverance:

- "I am resilient and handle stress with confidence."

- "I persevere through challenges with determination and strength."

- "I am committed to my goals and overcome obstacles with resilience."

3. Integrate Affirmations into Your Daily Routine:

CONSISTENCY IS KEY to making affirmations effective. Integrate your resilience and perseverance affirmations into your daily routine to reinforce positive beliefs about your ability to overcome challenges.

Steps for Integrating Affirmations into Your Daily Routine:

1. MORNING RITUAL: Start your day with resilience and perseverance affirmations to set a positive tone. Repeat them while getting ready, during your morning commute, or as part of your morning meditation.

2. Throughout the Day: Use reminders, such as sticky notes or phone alarms, to practice your affirmations throughout the day. Take short breaks to repeat your affirmations and refocus your mind.

3. Evening Reflection: End your day with affirmations to reinforce positive beliefs before sleep. Reflect on the challenges you faced during the day and use affirmations to acknowledge your resilience and perseverance.

4. Visualize Resilience and Perseverance:

VISUALIZATION CAN ENHANCE the impact of your affirmations. Imagine yourself embodying resilience and perseverance in the face of challenges. This helps to create a vivid mental image of strength and determination and reinforces your positive beliefs.

Steps for Visualizing Resilience and Perseverance:

1. FIND A QUIET SPACE: Find a quiet and comfortable space where you can relax and focus on your visualization.

2. Close Your Eyes: Close your eyes and take a few deep breaths to center yourself.

3. Visualize Your Affirmations: Visualize yourself living out your resilience and perseverance affirmations. See yourself handling stress with confidence, persevering through challenges, and maintaining a positive attitude. Imagine how it feels to embody these qualities and achieve your goals.

4. Engage Your Senses: Engage your senses in the visualization. What do you see, hear, feel, and even smell in this scenario? The more vivid the visualization, the more powerful it becomes.

5. Practice Self-Compassion:

SELF-COMPASSION IS essential for building resilience and perseverance. It involves treating yourself with the same kindness and understanding that you would offer to a friend.

Steps for Practicing Self-Compassion with Affirmations:

1. ACKNOWLEDGE YOUR Feelings: Recognize and validate your feelings about challenges and setbacks without judgment. Use affirmations to stay compassionate, such as "I am kind and gentle with myself as I navigate challenges."

2. Use Compassionate Affirmations: Create affirmations that promote self-compassion and understanding. For example, "I forgive myself for any mistakes and embrace growth" or "I am patient and understanding with myself during difficult times."

3. Practice Regularly: Integrate self-compassionate affirmations into your daily routine. Use them during moments of self-doubt or when you catch yourself engaging in negative self-talk.

Examples of Self-Compassionate Affirmations:

- "I AM KIND AND GENTLE with myself as I navigate challenges."

- "I forgive myself for any mistakes and embrace growth."

- "I am patient and understanding with myself during difficult times."

Inspirational Stories of Overcoming Adversity Through Affirmations

PERSONAL STORIES OF overcoming adversity can provide powerful inspiration and motivation. Here are a few real-life examples of individuals who have used affirmations to overcome significant challenges and achieve success.

1. Jennifer's Journey to Overcoming Fear of Public Speaking:

JENNIFER ALWAYS STRUGGLED with a fear of public speaking, which hindered her career advancement. She felt anxious and self-conscious whenever she had to speak in front of a group. Determined to overcome her fear, Jennifer decided to use affirmations to build her confidence and develop her public speaking skills.

Jennifer's Affirmation Practice:

JENNIFER CREATED AFFIRMATIONS that focused on her confidence and public speaking abilities, such as "I am confident and articulate when speaking in front of others," "I embrace public speaking as an opportunity to share my ideas," and "I speak with clarity and confidence."

Steps Jennifer Took:

1. DAILY PRACTICE: Jennifer integrated her affirmations into her daily routine. She repeated them every morning and evening, as well as before any public speaking engagements.

2. Visualization: Jennifer visualized herself speaking confidently and effectively in front of an audience. She imagined feeling calm, composed, and articulate.

3. Public Speaking Courses: Jennifer enrolled in public speaking courses and workshops to improve her skills and gain practical experience.

4. Seeking Support: Jennifer sought feedback and encouragement from friends, colleagues, and mentors who provided constructive criticism and support.

Jennifer's Transformation:

THROUGH CONSISTENT affirmation practice and dedicated effort, Jennifer gained the confidence to speak in front of groups. She successfully delivered presentations, participated in meetings, and even took on leadership roles that required public speaking. Jennifer's transformation highlighted the power of affirmations in overcoming fear and building confidence.

2. Robert's Path to Overcoming Career Setbacks:

ROBERT EXPERIENCED several career setbacks, including job loss and rejection from potential employers. These setbacks affected his confidence and motivation. Determined to overcome these challenges and achieve career success, Robert decided to use affirmations to build resilience and stay motivated.

Robert's Affirmation Practice:

ROBERT CREATED AFFIRMATIONS that focused on his career resilience and success, such as "I am resilient and bounce back from setbacks with confidence," "I attract career opportunities and success with my positive mindset," and "I am confident in my skills and abilities."

Steps Robert Took:

1. MORNING RITUAL: Robert started his day with career resilience affirmations to set a positive tone and boost his motivation.

2. Visualization: Robert visualized himself overcoming career setbacks, finding new job opportunities, and achieving success in his career.

3. Job Search Strategy: Robert developed a detailed job search strategy, including updating his resume, networking, and applying for jobs.

4. Seeking Support: Robert sought support from career coaches, mentors, and job search groups who provided guidance and encouragement.

Robert's Transformation:

THROUGH CONSISTENT affirmation practice and dedicated effort, Robert regained his confidence and resilience. He successfully navigated the job search process, secured a new job, and achieved career success. Robert's transformation highlighted the power of affirmations in overcoming career setbacks and building resilience.

3. Maria's Journey to Overcoming Health Challenges:

MARIA FACED SIGNIFICANT health challenges, including a chronic illness that affected her daily life. She felt overwhelmed and struggled to stay positive. Determined to improve her health and well-being, Maria decided to use affirmations to build resilience and maintain a positive mindset.

Maria's Affirmation Practice:

MARIA CREATED AFFIRMATIONS that focused on her health and well-being, such as "I am resilient and overcome health challenges with strength," "I am committed to my health and well-being," and "I am grateful for my body's ability to heal and recover."

Steps Maria Took:

1. DAILY PRACTICE: Maria integrated her affirmations into her daily routine. She repeated them every morning and evening, as well as during moments of health-related stress.

2. Visualization: Maria visualized herself feeling healthy, strong, and energetic. She imagined her body healing and recovering.

3. Health Plan: Maria developed a detailed health plan, including medical treatments, a healthy diet, exercise, and self-care practices.

4. Seeking Support: Maria sought support from healthcare professionals, support groups, and loved ones who provided guidance and encouragement.

Maria's Transformation:

THROUGH CONSISTENT affirmation practice and dedicated effort, Maria improved her health and well-being. She successfully managed her chronic illness, regained her strength, and maintained a positive mindset. Maria's transformation highlighted the power of affirmations in overcoming health challenges and building resilience.

4. David's Path to Overcoming Financial Difficulties:

DAVID FACED SIGNIFICANT financial difficulties, including debt and financial insecurity. He felt overwhelmed and struggled to stay positive about his financial future. Determined to improve his financial situation, David decided to use affirmations to build resilience and attract financial success.

David's Affirmation Practice:

DAVID CREATED AFFIRMATIONS that focused on his financial resilience and abundance, such as "I am resilient and overcome financial challenges with confidence," "I attract financial opportunities and success with my positive mindset," and "I am financially secure and confident in my ability to manage my finances."

Steps David Took:

1. MORNING RITUAL: David started his day with financial resilience affirmations to set a positive tone and boost his motivation.

2. Visualization: David visualized himself overcoming financial difficulties, managing his finances effectively, and achieving financial success.

3. Financial Plan: David developed a detailed financial plan, including budgeting, saving, and debt repayment strategies.

4. Seeking Support: David sought advice from financial advisors and joined financial support groups for guidance and encouragement.

David's Transformation:

THROUGH CONSISTENT affirmation practice and dedicated effort, David improved his financial situation. He successfully managed his finances, reduced his debt, and achieved financial security. David's transformation highlighted the power of affirmations in overcoming financial difficulties and building resilience.

Conclusion

Affirmations are powerful tools for facing and overcoming challenges, building resilience and perseverance, and achieving success in the face of adversity. By cultivating a positive and empowered mindset, overcoming self-doubt and fear, and reinforcing your commitment to your goals, affirmations can help you navigate life's obstacles with strength and determination.

In this chapter, we explored how to use affirmations to face and overcome challenges, build resilience and perseverance, and shared inspirational stories of overcoming adversity through affirmations. These stories demonstrate the profound impact affirmations can have on individuals' lives, providing inspiration and motivation for your own journey.

As you continue to practice affirmations for overcoming obstacles, remember to be patient and consistent. Positive change takes time, but with dedication and perseverance, you can harness the power of affirmations to transform your life and achieve your goals.

In the following chapters, we will explore specific areas where affirmations can make a significant impact, providing you with the tools and inspiration to harness the full potential of positive thinking.

Chapter 12: Creating a Customized Affirmation Plan

Affirmations are powerful tools for personal growth and development, but to maximize their effectiveness, it's essential to create a customized affirmation plan that aligns with your unique needs and goals. This chapter will guide you through the process of assessing your needs, designing a personalized affirmation plan, and providing tips for tracking your progress and staying motivated.

Assessing Your Needs and Goals

BEFORE YOU CAN CREATE a customized affirmation plan, you need to have a clear understanding of your needs and goals. This assessment will help you identify the areas of your life where affirmations can be most beneficial and the specific outcomes you want to achieve.

Steps for Assessing Your Needs and Goals:

1. REFLECT ON DIFFERENT Areas of Your Life:

Take some time to reflect on various aspects of your life, including personal development, career, relationships, health, and finances. Consider the following questions to guide your reflection:

- What areas of my life are going well, and where do I face challenges?

- What specific outcomes do I want to achieve in each area?

- What are my short-term and long-term goals?

2. Identify Your Strengths and Weaknesses:

Understanding your strengths and weaknesses can help you leverage your strengths and address areas for improvement. Consider the following questions:

- What are my core strengths, and how can they help me achieve my goals?

- What are my weaknesses, and how can I work on improving them?

3. Determine Your Values and Priorities:

Your values and priorities play a crucial role in shaping your goals and actions. Reflect on the following questions:

- What values are most important to me, and how do they influence my goals?

- What are my top priorities in life, and how can affirmations help me align with them?

4. Set Specific, Measurable, Achievable, Relevant, and Time-bound (SMART) Goals:

SMART goals provide a clear and structured framework for setting and achieving your objectives. Consider the following questions:

- What specific goals do I want to achieve in each area of my life?

- How will I measure my progress and success?

- Are my goals realistic and achievable within the given timeframe?

- How are my goals relevant to my overall values and priorities?

- What is the timeline for achieving my goals?

Examples of SMART Goals:

- PERSONAL DEVELOPMENT: "I will read one personal development book each month for the next six months to enhance my knowledge and skills."

- Career: "I will complete a professional certification course within the next year to advance my career prospects."

- Health: "I will exercise for at least 30 minutes, five days a week, to improve my physical fitness and overall well-being."

Designing a Personalized Affirmation Plan

ONCE YOU HAVE ASSESSED your needs and goals, the next step is to design a personalized affirmation plan that aligns with your unique aspirations. This plan will include specific affirmations, a routine for practicing them, and strategies for maximizing their impact.

Steps for Designing a Personalized Affirmation Plan:

1. Create Specific Affirmations for Each Goal:

BASED ON YOUR IDENTIFIED needs and goals, create affirmations that are positive, specific, and focused on the desired outcomes. Ensure that your affirmations reflect your values and priorities.

Steps for Creating Specific Affirmations:

- REFRAME NEGATIVE BELIEFS: Identify any negative beliefs related to your goals and reframe them into positive affirmations. For example, if you believe "I can't achieve my career goals," reframe it to "I am capable of achieving my career goals with determination and effort."

- Use Positive Language: Use positive and empowering language that affirms your ability to achieve your goals. Avoid using words like "not" or "don't."

- Be Specific: Make your affirmations specific to the outcomes you want to achieve. For instance, instead of saying "I am successful," say "I successfully complete my certification course and advance my career."

Examples of Specific Affirmations:

- PERSONAL DEVELOPMENT: "I am committed to continuous learning and read one personal development book each month."

- Career: "I am dedicated to advancing my career and complete my professional certification course within the next year."

- Health: "I prioritize my health and exercise for at least 30 minutes, five days a week."

2. Establish a Routine for Practicing Affirmations:

CONSISTENCY IS KEY to making affirmations effective. Establish a routine for practicing your affirmations daily. Consider incorporating them into your morning and evening routines, as well as throughout the day.

Steps for Establishing an Affirmation Routine:

- MORNING RITUAL: START your day with affirmations to set a positive tone. Repeat them while getting ready, during your morning commute, or as part of your morning meditation.

- Throughout the Day: Use reminders, such as sticky notes or phone alarms, to practice your affirmations throughout the day. Take short breaks to repeat your affirmations and refocus your mind.

- Evening Reflection: End your day with affirmations to reinforce positive beliefs before sleep. Reflect on your goals and use affirmations to acknowledge your progress and commitment.

3. Incorporate Visualization and Emotional Engagement:

VISUALIZATION AND EMOTIONAL engagement can enhance the impact of your affirmations. Imagine yourself achieving your goals and embodying the qualities you affirm. Engage your emotions to create a strong mental and emotional connection to your affirmations.

Steps for Incorporating Visualization and Emotional Engagement:

- FIND A QUIET SPACE: Find a quiet and comfortable space where you can relax and focus on your visualization.

- Close Your Eyes: Close your eyes and take a few deep breaths to center yourself.

- Visualize Your Affirmations: Visualize yourself living out your affirmations. See yourself achieving your goals, feeling accomplished, and embodying the qualities you affirm. Imagine how it feels to achieve your goals and embody these qualities.

- Engage Your Senses: Engage your senses in the visualization. What do you see, hear, feel, and even smell in this scenario? The more vivid the visualization, the more powerful it becomes.

4. Integrate Affirmations into Different Activities:

INTEGRATE YOUR AFFIRMATIONS into various activities throughout your day to reinforce positive beliefs and stay focused on your goals. Consider incorporating affirmations into activities such as exercise, journaling, and meditation.

Steps for Integrating Affirmations into Activities:

- EXERCISE: REPEAT YOUR affirmations while exercising to boost motivation and focus. For example, "I am strong and capable, and I achieve my fitness goals with determination."

- Journaling: Write your affirmations in a journal and reflect on their impact. For example, "Today, I reaffirm my commitment to continuous learning and personal growth."

- Meditation: Integrate affirmations into your meditation practice to deepen your focus and emotional connection. For example, "I am calm, centered, and focused on achieving my goals."

5. Seek Support and Accountability:

SHARING YOUR GOALS and affirmations with supportive friends, family members, or a mentor can provide encouragement and accountability. Consider joining a group or community focused on personal development to share experiences and gain insights.

Steps for Seeking Support and Accountability:

- SHARE YOUR GOALS: Share your goals and affirmations with trusted individuals who can provide support and encouragement. For example, “I am working on improving my public speaking skills, and I use affirmations to build my confidence.”

- Join a Group: Consider joining a personal development group or online community to share experiences and gain insights. For example, “I am part of a personal development group where we share our goals and support each other's growth.”

- Seek a Mentor: Find a mentor who can provide guidance and accountability on your personal development journey. For example, “I have a mentor who helps me stay focused on my goals and provides valuable feedback.”

Tips for Tracking Progress and Staying Motivated

TRACKING YOUR PROGRESS and staying motivated are essential components of a successful affirmation plan. Regularly assessing your achievements, celebrating milestones, and maintaining a positive mindset can help you stay on track and achieve your goals.

Steps for Tracking Progress and Staying Motivated:

1. Keep a Progress Journal:

MAINTAIN A JOURNAL to track your progress, reflect on your experiences, and document your achievements. Use your journal to record your affirmations, set milestones, and celebrate your successes.

Steps for Keeping a Progress Journal:

- SET REGULAR CHECK-Ins: Set aside regular times to reflect on your progress and update your journal. For example, "Every Sunday evening, I review my progress and update my journal."

- Document Achievements: Record your achievements and milestones in your journal. For example, "This week, I successfully completed a major project at work and received positive feedback from my manager."

- Reflect on Challenges: Reflect on any challenges you faced and how you overcame them. For example, "I faced a setback in my fitness routine, but I used affirmations to stay motivated and got back on track."

2. Celebrate Milestones and Achievements:

CELEBRATING YOUR MILESTONES and achievements can boost motivation and reinforce your commitment to your goals. Acknowledge your efforts and reward yourself for your progress.

Steps for Celebrating Milestones and Achievements:

- SET MILESTONES: BREAK down your goals into smaller, manageable milestones. For example, "I will celebrate completing each chapter of my personal development book."

- Acknowledge Your Efforts: Take time to acknowledge and celebrate your efforts and achievements. For example, "I am proud of my progress and celebrate my achievements with gratitude."

- Reward Yourself: Reward yourself for reaching milestones and achieving goals. For example, "I will treat myself to a relaxing spa day after completing my certification course."

3. Stay Positive and Motivated:

MAINTAINING A POSITIVE mindset and staying motivated are crucial for achieving your goals. Use affirmations to reinforce your commitment, build confidence, and stay focused on your aspirations.

Steps for Staying Positive and Motivated:

- USE POSITIVE AFFIRMATIONS: Regularly practice positive affirmations that reinforce your commitment and motivation.

For example, "I am motivated and committed to achieving my goals."

- Visualize Success: Visualize yourself achieving your goals and experiencing success. For example, "I see myself successfully completing my goals and feeling accomplished and fulfilled."

- Practice Self-Compassion: Be kind and gentle with yourself, especially during setbacks. Use affirmations to practice self-compassion, such as "I am patient and understanding with myself as I navigate challenges."

4. Adjust Your Plan as Needed:

FLEXIBILITY IS ESSENTIAL for staying on track and achieving your goals. Be open to adjusting your affirmation plan based on your progress and changing circumstances.

Steps for Adjusting Your Plan:

- REGULARLY ASSESS PROGRESS: Regularly assess your progress and determine if any adjustments are needed. For example, "Every month, I review my progress and adjust my plan if necessary."

- Stay Flexible: Be open to making changes to your affirmation plan based on your needs and goals. For example, "I am flexible and adapt my plan to stay aligned with my goals."

- Seek Feedback: Seek feedback from supportive individuals to gain insights and make informed adjustments. For example, "I seek feedback from my mentor to refine my affirmation plan and stay focused on my goals."

5. Maintain Accountability:

ACCOUNTABILITY CAN help you stay committed and focused on your goals. Share your progress with supportive individuals who can provide encouragement and hold you accountable.

Steps for Maintaining Accountability:

- SHARE YOUR PROGRESS: Share your progress with trusted friends, family members, or a mentor. For example, "I regularly update my accountability partner on my progress and achievements."

- Join an Accountability Group: Consider joining an accountability group or community focused on personal development. For example, "I am part of an accountability group where we share our goals and support each other's progress."

- Set Regular Check-Ins: Set regular check-ins with your accountability partner or group to review your progress and stay motivated. For example, "I have weekly check-ins with my accountability partner to review my progress and stay on track."

Example of a Customized Affirmation Plan

TO ILLUSTRATE HOW TO create a customized affirmation plan, let's consider an example of an individual named Alex who wants to improve his overall well-being, advance his career, and enhance his relationships.

1. Assessing Needs and Goals:

ALEX REFLECTS ON DIFFERENT areas of his life and identifies his needs and goals:

- Personal Development: Improve overall well-being and build healthy habits.

- Career: Advance to a leadership position within the next year.

- Relationships: Strengthen communication and emotional intimacy with his partner.

2. Creating Specific Affirmations:

Based on his goals, Alex creates specific affirmations for each area:

- Personal Development: "I am committed to my well-being and build healthy habits that enhance my life."

- Career: "I am dedicated to advancing my career and successfully secure a leadership position within the next year."

- Relationships: "I communicate openly and effectively with my partner, strengthening our emotional intimacy."

3. Establishing a Routine for Practicing Affirmations:

Alex establishes a routine for practicing his affirmations:

- Morning Ritual: Alex starts his day with affirmations while getting ready and during his morning commute.

- Throughout the Day: Alex uses sticky notes and phone alarms to remind him to practice affirmations during breaks.

- Evening Reflection: Alex ends his day with affirmations, reflecting on his goals and progress before sleep.

4. Incorporating Visualization and Emotional Engagement:

Alex incorporates visualization and emotional engagement into his affirmation practice:

- Visualization: Alex finds a quiet space, closes his eyes, and visualizes himself living out his affirmations, achieving his goals, and feeling accomplished.

- Emotional Engagement: Alex engages his emotions during visualization, imagining the positive feelings associated with achieving his goals.

5. Integrating Affirmations into Different Activities:

Alex integrates his affirmations into various activities:

- Exercise: Alex repeats his affirmations while jogging to boost motivation.

- Journaling: Alex writes his affirmations in a journal and reflects on their impact.

- Meditation: Alex integrates affirmations into his meditation practice to deepen focus.

6. Seeking Support and Accountability:

Alex seeks support and accountability:

- Sharing Goals: Alex shares his goals and affirmations with his partner and a trusted mentor.

- Joining a Group: Alex joins a personal development group where members share goals and support each other.

- Seeking a Mentor: Alex finds a mentor who provides guidance and accountability.

7. Tracking Progress and Staying Motivated:

Alex tracks his progress and stays motivated:

- Progress Journal: Alex maintains a journal to track his progress, reflect on experiences, and document achievements.

- Celebrating Milestones: Alex sets milestones, acknowledges efforts, and rewards himself for achievements.

- Staying Positive: Alex uses positive affirmations, visualizes success, and practices self-compassion.

- Adjusting Plan: Alex regularly assesses progress, stays flexible, seeks feedback, and makes adjustments as needed.

- Maintaining Accountability: Alex shares progress with his accountability partner, joins an accountability group, and sets regular check-ins.

Example of Alex's Customized Affirmation Plan:

Personal Development:

- GOALS: IMPROVE OVERALL well-being and build healthy habits.

- Affirmations: "I am committed to my well-being and build healthy habits that enhance my life."

- Routine: Morning ritual, reminders throughout the day, evening reflection.

- Visualization: Imagine living a healthy lifestyle and feeling energized and vibrant.

- Activities: Repeat affirmations during exercise, write in a journal, integrate into meditation.

- Support: Share goals with partner and mentor, join a personal development group.

- Tracking: Maintain a progress journal, set milestones, celebrate achievements, stay positive, adjust plan, maintain accountability.

***Career*:**

- Goals: Advance to a leadership position within the next year.

- Affirmations: "I am dedicated to advancing my career and successfully secure a leadership position within the next year."

- Routine: Morning ritual, reminders throughout the day, evening reflection.

- Visualization: Imagine achieving a leadership position, feeling confident and successful.

- Activities: Repeat affirmations during breaks, write in a journal, integrate into meditation.

- Support: Share goals with mentor, join a professional development group.

- Tracking: Maintain a progress journal, set milestones, celebrate achievements, stay positive, adjust plan, maintain accountability.

Relationships:

- Goals: Strengthen communication and emotional intimacy with partner.

- Affirmations: "I communicate openly and effectively with my partner, strengthening our emotional intimacy."

- Routine: Morning ritual, reminders throughout the day, evening reflection.

- Visualization: Imagine having open and meaningful conversations with partner, feeling connected and loved.

- Activities: Repeat affirmations during breaks, write in a journal, integrate into meditation.

- Support: Share goals with partner, join a relationship-focused group.

- Tracking: Maintain a progress journal, set milestones, celebrate achievements, stay positive, adjust plan, maintain accountability.

Conclusion

Creating a customized affirmation plan is a powerful way to align your affirmations with your unique needs and goals, ensuring maximum effectiveness. By assessing your needs, designing a personalized plan, and tracking your progress, you can harness the power of affirmations to achieve personal growth, enhance well-being, and realize your aspirations.

In this chapter, we explored how to assess your needs and goals, design a personalized affirmation plan, and provided tips for tracking progress and staying motivated. By integrating affirmations into your daily routine, incorporating visualization and emotional engagement, seeking support, and maintaining accountability, you can create a customized affirmation plan that empowers you to overcome challenges and achieve success.

As you continue to practice affirmations and work towards your goals, remember to be patient and consistent. Positive change takes time, but with dedication and perseverance, you can harness the power of affirmations to transform your life and achieve your dreams. In the following chapters, we will explore specific areas where affirmations can make a significant impact, providing you with the tools and inspiration to harness the full potential of positive thinking.

Chapter 13: The Role of Visualization and Meditation

Visualization and meditation are powerful practices that can significantly enhance the effectiveness of affirmations. By combining these techniques, you can deepen your mental and emotional connection to your affirmations, making them more impactful and transformative. This chapter will explore how to enhance affirmations with visualization techniques, incorporate meditation into your affirmation practice, and provide guided visualization exercises to reinforce your affirmations.

Enhancing Affirmations with Visualization Techniques

VISUALIZATION IS THE practice of creating vivid mental images of your desired outcomes and experiences. When combined with affirmations, visualization can help you embody the qualities and achievements you affirm, reinforcing your belief in their possibility and reality.

Understanding the Power of Visualization:

VISUALIZATION WORKS by harnessing the power of your imagination to create a mental picture of your goals and desires. This process engages your subconscious mind, helping to align your thoughts, emotions, and actions with your affirmations. By repeatedly visualizing your desired outcomes, you can strengthen your belief in your ability to achieve them and increase your motivation to take action.

The Role of Visualization in Enhancing Affirmations:

VISUALIZATION CAN HELP you:

- Deepen your emotional connection to your affirmations

- Strengthen your belief in the possibility of your affirmations

- Increase motivation and focus on your goals

- Create a clear mental image of success

- Reinforce positive beliefs and behaviors

Steps for Enhancing Affirmations with Visualization:

1. Create Vivid Mental Images:

BEGIN BY CREATING VIVID mental images of your desired outcomes and experiences. These images should be detailed and specific, reflecting the qualities and achievements you affirm.

Steps for Creating Vivid Mental Images:

1. IDENTIFY YOUR DESIRED Outcomes: Reflect on your affirmations and identify the specific outcomes you want to achieve. For example, if your affirmation is "I am confident and successful in my career," visualize yourself achieving career success and feeling confident.

2. Engage Your Senses: Use all your senses to create a vivid mental image. What do you see, hear, feel, smell, and even taste in this scenario? The more detailed and sensory-rich the image, the more powerful it becomes.

3. Focus on Positive Emotions: Pay attention to the positive emotions associated with achieving your desired outcomes. How does it feel to achieve your goals and embody your affirmations? Focus on these emotions to deepen your connection to your visualization.

2. Integrate Visualization into Your Affirmation Practice:

INTEGRATE VISUALIZATION into your daily affirmation practice to reinforce your beliefs and goals. This can be done through dedicated visualization sessions or by incorporating visualization into your existing routines.

Steps for Integrating Visualization into Your Affirmation Practice:

1. MORNING VISUALIZATION: Start your day with a visualization session to set a positive tone. Spend a few minutes visualizing your desired outcomes while repeating your affirmations. For example, "I see myself achieving career success and feeling confident and accomplished."

2. Throughout the Day: Use short visualization breaks throughout the day to reinforce your affirmations. Close your eyes, take a few deep breaths, and visualize your desired outcomes. For example, "I see myself confidently presenting at a meeting and receiving positive feedback."

3. Evening Reflection: End your day with a visualization session to reinforce positive beliefs before sleep. Reflect on your affirmations and visualize your desired outcomes. For example, "I see myself achieving my goals and feeling fulfilled and content."

3. Use Visualization Tools and Techniques:

THERE ARE VARIOUS TOOLS and techniques that can enhance your visualization practice. Experiment with different methods to find what works best for you.

Visualization Tools and Techniques:

- VISION BOARDS: CREATE a vision board with images and words that represent your goals and affirmations. Place it somewhere you can see it regularly to reinforce your visualization.

- Guided Imagery: Use guided imagery recordings or apps that lead you through a visualization process. These can provide structure and help you create more vivid mental images.

- *Creative Visualization: Engage in creative activities such as drawing, painting, or writing to represent your desired outcomes. This can help you connect with your visualization on a deeper level.

Incorporating Meditation into Your Affirmation Practice

MEDITATION IS A PRACTICE that involves focusing your mind and achieving a state of calm and clarity. When combined with affirmations, meditation can help you deepen your mental and emotional connection to your affirmations, reduce stress, and enhance overall well-being.

Understanding the Benefits of Meditation:

MEDITATION OFFERS NUMEROUS benefits, including reducing stress, improving focus, enhancing emotional regulation, and promoting overall well-being. When practiced regularly, meditation can help you cultivate a calm and centered mindset, making it easier to connect with your affirmations.

The Role of Meditation in Enhancing Affirmations:

MEDITATION CAN HELP you:

- Deepen your mental and emotional connection to your affirmations

- Reduce stress and create a state of calm and clarity

- Improve focus and concentration on your goals

- Enhance self-awareness and mindfulness

- Reinforce positive beliefs and behaviors

Steps for Incorporating Meditation into Your Affirmation Practice:

1. Choose a Meditation Technique:

THERE ARE VARIOUS MEDITATION techniques that can complement your affirmation practice. Choose a technique that resonates with you and supports your goals.

Common Meditation Techniques:

- MINDFULNESS MEDITATION: Focus on your breath and observe your thoughts and sensations without judgment. This can help you cultivate mindfulness and awareness.

- Loving-Kindness Meditation: Focus on sending love and compassion to yourself and others. This can help you cultivate positive emotions and reinforce affirmations related to self-love and compassion.

- Guided Meditation: Use guided meditation recordings or apps that lead you through a meditation process. This can provide structure and help you stay focused.

2. Create a Meditation Routine:

ESTABLISH A REGULAR meditation routine that includes your affirmations. This can be done through dedicated meditation sessions or by incorporating meditation into your existing routines.

Steps for Creating a Meditation Routine:

1. MORNING MEDITATION: Start your day with a meditation session to set a positive tone. Spend a few minutes meditating and repeating your affirmations. For example, "I am calm, centered, and focused on achieving my goals."

2. Throughout the Day: Use short meditation breaks throughout the day to reinforce your affirmations. Close your eyes, take a few deep breaths, and meditate on your affirmations. For example, "I am resilient and handle stress with confidence."

3. Evening Meditation: End your day with a meditation session to reinforce positive beliefs before sleep. Reflect on your affirmations and meditate on your desired outcomes. For example, "I am grateful for my progress and continue to move forward with confidence."

3. Combine Meditation with Visualization:

COMBINING MEDITATION with visualization can enhance the impact of both practices. Use meditation to create a state of calm and clarity, and then visualize your desired outcomes while repeating your affirmations.

Steps for Combining Meditation with Visualization:

1. FIND A QUIET SPACE: Find a quiet and comfortable space where you can relax and focus on your meditation and visualization.

2. Meditate to Create Calm: Start with a few minutes of meditation to create a state of calm and clarity. Focus on your breath and let go of any tension or stress.

3. Visualize Your Affirmations: Transition into visualization while maintaining a meditative state. Visualize your desired outcomes and repeat your affirmations. For example, "I see myself achieving my goals and feeling fulfilled and content."

4. Engage Your Senses: Engage your senses in the visualization. What do you see, hear, feel, and even smell in this scenario? The more vivid the visualization, the more powerful it becomes.

4. Use Guided Meditation and Visualization Exercises:

GUIDED MEDITATION AND visualization exercises can provide structure and support for your practice. These exercises can help you create more vivid mental images and deepen your connection to your affirmations.

Examples of Guided Meditation and Visualization Exercises:

Exercise 1: Morning Affirmation Meditation

1. FIND A QUIET SPACE: Find a quiet and comfortable space where you can sit or lie down.

2. Focus on Your Breath: Close your eyes and take a few deep breaths. Focus on the sensation of your breath entering and leaving your body.

3. Repeat Your Affirmations: Begin repeating your affirmations silently or aloud. For example, "I am confident, capable, and successful."

4. Visualize Your Desired Outcomes: As you repeat your affirmations, visualize your desired outcomes. See yourself achieving your goals and embodying the qualities you affirm.

5. Engage Your Senses: Engage your senses in the visualization. What do you see, hear, feel, and even smell in this scenario?

6. Feel the Emotions: Focus on the positive emotions associated with achieving your goals. How does it feel to achieve your goals and embody your affirmations?

7. Conclude the Meditation: After a few minutes, gently bring your awareness back to your breath. Take a few deep breaths and slowly open your eyes. Reflect on the positive feelings and carry them with you throughout the day.

Exercise 2: Evening Reflection Meditation

1. FIND A QUIET SPACE: Find a quiet and comfortable space where you can sit or lie down.

2. Focus on Your Breath: Close your eyes and take a few deep breaths. Focus on the sensation of your breath entering and leaving your body.

3. Reflect on Your Day: Spend a few moments reflecting on your day. Acknowledge any challenges you faced and any progress you made towards your goals.

4. Repeat Your Affirmations: Begin repeating your affirmations silently or aloud. For example, "I am resilient, determined, and capable of achieving my goals."

5. Visualize Your Desired Outcomes: As you repeat your affirmations, visualize your desired outcomes. See yourself achieving your goals and embodying the qualities you affirm.

6. Engage Your Senses: Engage your senses in the visualization. What do you see, hear, feel, and even smell in this scenario?

7. Feel the Emotions: Focus on the positive emotions associated with achieving your goals. How does it feel to achieve your goals and embody your affirmations?

8. Conclude the Meditation: After a few minutes, gently bring your awareness back to your breath. Take a few deep breaths and slowly open your eyes. Reflect on the positive feelings and carry them with you as you prepare for sleep.

Exercise 3: Guided Visualization for Goal Achievement

1. FIND A QUIET SPACE: Find a quiet and comfortable space where you can sit or lie down.

2. Focus on Your Breath: Close your eyes and take a few deep breaths. Focus on the sensation of your breath entering and leaving your body.

3. Begin the Guided Visualization: Imagine yourself standing at the beginning of a path that leads to your desired goal. See the path clearly and visualize yourself taking the first step.

4. Visualize the Journey: As you walk along the path, visualize the steps you take to achieve your goal. See yourself overcoming obstacles, staying focused, and making progress.

5. Engage Your Senses: Engage your senses in the visualization. What do you see, hear, feel, and even smell along the path?

6. Visualize the Outcome: As you reach the end of the path, visualize yourself achieving your goal. See yourself celebrating your success and feeling proud and accomplished.

7. Feel the Emotions: Focus on the positive emotions associated with achieving your goal. How does it feel to achieve your goal and embody your affirmations?

8. Conclude the Visualization: After a few minutes, gently bring your awareness back to your breath. Take a few deep breaths and slowly open your eyes. Reflect on the positive feelings and carry them with you as you work towards your goal.

Combining Visualization and Meditation with Affirmations: A Case Study

TO ILLUSTRATE THE IMPACT of combining visualization and meditation with affirmations, let's consider the example of Sarah, a marketing professional who wants to improve her public speaking skills and advance her career.

Assessing Needs and Goals:

SARAH REFLECTS ON HER professional goals and identifies her need to improve public speaking skills to advance her career. She sets a specific goal of confidently delivering presentations and securing a leadership position within the next year.

Creating Specific Affirmations:

BASED ON HER GOAL, Sarah creates specific affirmations:

- "I am confident and articulate when speaking in front of others."

- "I embrace public speaking as an opportunity to share my ideas."

- "I am dedicated to advancing my career and successfully secure a leadership position within the next year."

Establishing a Routine for Practicing Affirmations:

SARAH ESTABLISHES A routine for practicing her affirmations:

- Morning Ritual: Sarah starts her day with affirmations while getting ready and during her morning commute.

- Throughout the Day: Sarah uses sticky notes and phone alarms to remind her to practice affirmations during breaks.

- Evening Reflection: Sarah ends her day with affirmations, reflecting on her progress and goals before sleep.

Integrating Visualization and Emotional Engagement:

SARAH INCORPORATES visualization and emotional engagement into her affirmation practice:

- Visualization: Sarah finds a quiet space, closes her eyes, and visualizes herself delivering confident and articulate presentations. She imagines the positive feedback from her audience and the sense of accomplishment.

- Emotional Engagement: Sarah focuses on the positive emotions associated with achieving her goal, such as confidence, pride, and excitement.

Incorporating Meditation into Affirmation Practice:

SARAH INCORPORATES meditation into her affirmation practice to deepen her mental and emotional connection:

- Morning Meditation: Sarah starts her day with a 10-minute mindfulness meditation followed by repeating her affirmations and visualizing her desired outcomes.

- Throughout the Day: Sarah takes short meditation breaks to focus on her breath, repeat her affirmations, and visualize her success.

- Evening Meditation: Sarah ends her day with a 10-minute reflection meditation, repeating her affirmations and visualizing her desired outcomes.

Using Guided Meditation and Visualization Exercises:

SARAH USES GUIDED MEDITATION and visualization exercises to support her practice:

- Morning Affirmation Meditation: Sarah follows a guided meditation that focuses on confidence and public speaking, repeating her affirmations and visualizing successful presentations.

- Evening Reflection Meditation: Sarah follows a guided reflection meditation, repeating her affirmations and visualizing her progress and achievements.

Tracking Progress and Staying Motivated:

SARAH TRACKS HER PROGRESS and stays motivated:

- Progress Journal: Sarah maintains a journal to track her progress, reflect on experiences, and document achievements.

- Celebrating Milestones: Sarah sets milestones, acknowledges efforts, and rewards herself for achievements, such as treating herself to a special dinner after delivering a successful presentation.

- Staying Positive: Sarah uses positive affirmations, visualizes success, and practices self-compassion to stay motivated and focused on her goals.

- Adjusting Plan: Sarah regularly assesses progress, stays flexible, seeks feedback from her mentor, and makes adjustments to her affirmation plan as needed.

- Maintaining Accountability: Sarah shares her progress with her accountability partner, joins a professional development group, and sets regular check-ins to review progress and stay motivated.

Sarah's Transformation:

THROUGH CONSISTENT practice of affirmations, visualization, and meditation, Sarah experiences significant improvements in her public speaking skills and career advancement. She confidently delivers presentations, receives positive feedback, and secures a leadership position within the next year. Sarah's transformation highlights the power of combining visualization and meditation with affirmations to achieve personal and professional goals.

Conclusion

Visualization and meditation are powerful practices that can significantly enhance the effectiveness of affirmations. By combining these techniques, you can deepen your mental and emotional connection to your affirmations, reduce stress, and enhance overall well-being. Visualization helps you create vivid mental images of your desired outcomes, while meditation creates a state of calm and clarity that supports your affirmation practice.

In this chapter, we explored how to enhance affirmations with visualization techniques, incorporate meditation into your affirmation practice, and provided guided visualization exercises to reinforce your affirmations. By integrating visualization and meditation into your daily routine, engaging your senses and emotions, and using guided exercises, you can create a powerful and transformative affirmation practice.

As you continue to practice affirmations, visualization, and meditation, remember to be patient and consistent. Positive change takes time, but with dedication and perseverance, you can harness the power of these techniques to transform your life and achieve your goals. In the following chapters, we will explore specific areas where affirmations can make a significant impact, providing you with the tools and inspiration to harness the full potential of positive thinking.

Chapter 14: Affirmations for a Fulfilling Life

Using Affirmations to Create a Balanced and Fulfilling Life

A fulfilling life is characterized by balance, joy, and a sense of purpose across various areas such as career, relationships, health, and personal growth. Affirmations can be powerful tools to help you achieve this balance and fulfillment by aligning your thoughts, beliefs, and actions with your deepest values and desires.

Understanding the Concept of a Fulfilling Life:

A FULFILLING LIFE IS one where you feel content, satisfied, and aligned with your values and goals. It involves finding joy and purpose in your daily activities, maintaining healthy relationships, achieving personal and professional goals, and taking care of your physical and mental well-being.

The Role of Affirmations in Creating a Fulfilling Life:

AFFIRMATIONS CAN HELP you:

- Cultivate a positive mindset and outlook on life

- Align your actions with your values and goals

- Foster a sense of balance and harmony across different areas of your life

- Increase motivation and resilience

- Enhance your overall sense of well-being and satisfaction

Steps for Using Affirmations to Create a Balanced and Fulfilling Life:

1. Define What Fulfillment Means to You:

BEGIN BY DEFINING WHAT a fulfilling life looks like for you. This involves identifying your core values, priorities, and the areas of your life that are most important to you.

Steps for Defining Fulfillment:

1. REFLECT ON YOUR Values and Priorities: Take some time to reflect on your core values and what matters most to you. Consider areas such as career, relationships, health, personal growth, and leisure. For example, "I value personal growth, strong relationships, and a healthy lifestyle."

2. Identify Key Areas of Focus: Identify the key areas of your life that contribute to your sense of fulfillment. These could include your career, family, friendships, health, hobbies, and personal development. For example, "I want to focus on improving my career, maintaining healthy relationships, and enhancing my physical fitness."

3. Set Specific Goals: Define clear and specific goals for each area of your life. For example, "I want to advance to a leadership position in my career," "I want to build deeper connections with my family and friends," and "I want to achieve a higher level of physical fitness."

2. Create Affirmations for Each Area of Your Life:

ONCE YOU HAVE DEFINED what fulfillment means to you, create affirmations that support your goals and aspirations in each area. Ensure that these affirmations are positive, specific, and reflect your desired outcomes.

Steps for Creating Affirmations:

1. REFRAME NEGATIVE Beliefs: Identify any negative beliefs related to each area of your life and reframe them into positive affirmations. For example, if you believe "I can't balance work and personal life," reframe it to "I am capable of balancing work and personal life with ease."

2. Use Positive Language: Use positive and empowering language that affirms your ability to achieve your goals. Avoid using words like "not" or "don't."

3. Be Specific: Make your affirmations specific to the outcomes you want to achieve. For instance, instead of saying "I am successful," say "I am successful in advancing my career and achieving my professional goals."

Examples of Affirmations for Different Areas of Life:

- CAREER: "I AM DEDICATED to advancing my career and achieving my professional goals."

- Relationships: "I build strong and meaningful connections with my family and friends."

- Health: "I prioritize my health and well-being, making choices that support a healthy lifestyle."

- Personal Growth: "I am committed to continuous learning and personal development."

- Leisure: "I make time for activities that bring me joy and relaxation."

3. Integrate Affirmations into Your Daily Routine:

Consistency is key to making affirmations effective. Integrate your affirmations into your daily routine to reinforce positive beliefs and stay focused on your goals.

Steps for Integrating Affirmations into Your Daily Routine:

1. MORNING RITUAL: Start your day with affirmations to set a positive tone. Repeat them while getting ready, during your morning commute, or as part of your morning meditation. For example, "I am dedicated to advancing my career and achieving my professional goals."

2. Throughout the Day: Use reminders, such as sticky notes or phone alarms, to practice your affirmations throughout the day. Take short breaks to repeat your affirmations and refocus your mind. For example, "I build strong and meaningful connections with my family and friends."

3. Evening Reflection: End your day with affirmations to reinforce positive beliefs before sleep. Reflect on your goals and use affirmations to acknowledge your progress and commitment. For example, "I prioritize my health and well-being, making choices that support a healthy lifestyle."

4. Incorporate Visualization and Emotional Engagement:

VISUALIZATION AND EMOTIONAL engagement can enhance the impact of your affirmations. Imagine yourself achieving your goals and embodying the qualities you affirm. Engage your emotions to create a strong mental and emotional connection to your affirmations.

Steps for Incorporating Visualization and Emotional Engagement:

1. FIND A QUIET SPACE: Find a quiet and comfortable space where you can relax and focus on your visualization.

2. Close Your Eyes: Close your eyes and take a few deep breaths to center yourself.

3. Visualize Your Affirmations: Visualize yourself living out your affirmations. See yourself achieving your goals, feeling fulfilled, and embodying the qualities you affirm. For example, "I see myself advancing in my career and feeling confident and accomplished."

4. Engage Your Senses: Engage your senses in the visualization. What do you see, hear, feel, and even smell in this scenario? The more vivid the visualization, the more powerful it becomes.

5. Feel the Emotions: Focus on the positive emotions associated with achieving your goals. How does it feel to achieve your goals and embody your affirmations? For example, "I feel joyful and connected as I build strong relationships with my family and friends."

5. Monitor Your Progress and Adjust as Needed:

REGULARLY MONITOR YOUR progress and adjust your affirmations and goals as needed. This will help you stay on track and ensure that your affirmations remain aligned with your values and aspirations.

Steps for Monitoring Progress and Adjusting:

1. SET REGULAR CHECK-Ins: Set aside regular times to reflect on your progress and update your affirmations and goals. For example, "Every Sunday evening, I review my progress and adjust my affirmations if necessary."

2. Celebrate Achievements: Acknowledge and celebrate your achievements and milestones. For example, "I am proud of my progress and celebrate my achievements with gratitude."

3. Adjust as Needed: Be open to adjusting your affirmations and goals based on your progress and changing circumstances. For example, "I am flexible and adapt my affirmations to stay aligned with my goals."

Integrating Affirmations into All Areas of Your Life

TO CREATE A BALANCED and fulfilling life, it's essential to integrate affirmations into all areas of your life. This holistic approach ensures that you address various aspects of your well-being and maintain harmony across different domains.

Steps for Integrating Affirmations into All Areas of Your Life:

1. Career and Professional Development:

AFFIRMATIONS CAN HELP you achieve your career goals, build confidence, and enhance your professional development.

Examples of Career Affirmations:

- "I AM DEDICATED TO advancing my career and achieving my professional goals."

- "I am confident and capable in my job, and I consistently perform at my best."

- "I attract opportunities for growth and success in my career."

2. Relationships and Social Connections:

AFFIRMATIONS CAN HELP you build and maintain strong, meaningful relationships with family, friends, and colleagues.

Examples of Relationship Affirmations:

- "I BUILD STRONG AND meaningful connections with my family and friends."

- "I communicate openly and effectively with those around me."

- "I am loving, compassionate, and supportive in my relationships."

3. Health and Well-Being:

AFFIRMATIONS CAN HELP you prioritize your health, adopt healthy habits, and enhance your overall well-being.

Examples of Health Affirmations:

- "I PRIORITIZE MY HEALTH and well-being, making choices that support a healthy lifestyle."

- "I am committed to regular exercise and a balanced diet to maintain my physical fitness."

- "I nurture my mental and emotional well-being through self-care and mindfulness."

4. Personal Growth and Development:

AFFIRMATIONS CAN HELP you stay committed to continuous learning and personal growth.

Examples of Personal Growth Affirmations:

- "I AM COMMITTED TO continuous learning and personal development."

- "I embrace challenges and see them as opportunities for growth."

- "I am confident in my ability to achieve my personal goals and aspirations."

5. Leisure and Hobbies:

AFFIRMATIONS CAN HELP you make time for activities that bring you joy and relaxation.

Examples of Leisure Affirmations:

- "I MAKE TIME FOR ACTIVITIES that bring me joy and relaxation."

- "I explore new hobbies and interests that enrich my life."

- "I balance work and leisure to maintain a fulfilling and joyful life."

6. Financial Stability and Abundance:

AFFIRMATIONS CAN HELP you achieve financial stability and attract abundance.

Examples of Financial Affirmations:

- "I AM FINANCIALLY stable and manage my finances wisely."

- "I attract abundance and prosperity into my life."

- "I am confident in my ability to achieve financial security and success."

7. Spirituality and Inner Peace:

AFFIRMATIONS CAN HELP you cultivate inner peace, mindfulness, and spiritual growth.

Examples of Spiritual Affirmations:

- "I AM AT PEACE WITH myself and the world around me."

- "I practice mindfulness and stay present in the moment."

- "I am connected to my inner wisdom and trust in my journey."

Real-Life Success Stories of Holistic Transformation

REAL-LIFE SUCCESS STORIES can provide powerful inspiration and motivation. Here are a few examples of individuals who have used affirmations to achieve holistic transformation and create a balanced and fulfilling life.

1. Emily's Journey to Work-Life Balance:

EMILY, A MARKETING executive, struggled with work-life balance, feeling overwhelmed by her job demands and neglecting her personal life. Determined to achieve a more balanced and fulfilling life, Emily decided to use affirmations to align her actions with her values and goals.

Emily's Affirmation Practice:

EMILY CREATED AFFIRMATIONS focused on work-life balance, personal growth, and relationships:

- "I am capable of balancing work and personal life with ease."

- "I prioritize my well-being and make time for activities that bring me joy."

- "I build strong and meaningful connections with my family and friends."

Steps Emily Took:

1. MORNING RITUAL: Emily started her day with affirmations while getting ready and during her morning commute.

2. Visualization: Emily visualized herself balancing work and personal life, feeling fulfilled and content.

3. Setting Boundaries: Emily set clear boundaries between work and personal time, ensuring she made time for self-care and relationships.

4. Seeking Support: Emily sought support from a mentor and joined a personal development group for guidance and accountability.

Emily's Transformation:

THROUGH CONSISTENT affirmation practice and dedicated effort, Emily achieved work-life balance and enhanced her overall well-being. She felt more fulfilled, maintained strong relationships, and performed better at work. Emily's transformation highlighted the power of affirmations in creating a balanced and fulfilling life.

2. Michael's Path to Personal and Professional Growth:

MICHAEL, A SOFTWARE engineer, wanted to advance his career while also focusing on personal growth and well-being. He felt stuck in his current role and lacked motivation for self-improvement. Determined to achieve his goals, Michael decided to use affirmations to stay focused and motivated.

Michael's Affirmation Practice:

MICHAEL CREATED AFFIRMATIONS focused on career advancement, personal growth, and health:

- "I am dedicated to advancing my career and achieving my professional goals."

- "I am committed to continuous learning and personal development."

- "I prioritize my health and well-being, making choices that support a healthy lifestyle."

Steps Michael Took:

1. MORNING RITUAL: Michael started his day with affirmations while getting ready and during his morning commute.

2. Visualization: Michael visualized himself achieving career success, feeling confident and accomplished.

3. Continuous Learning: Michael enrolled in professional development courses and pursued new certifications.

4. Healthy Habits: Michael adopted healthy habits such as regular exercise and a balanced diet.

Michael's Transformation:

THROUGH CONSISTENT affirmation practice and dedicated effort, Michael achieved career advancement, personal growth, and enhanced well-being. He secured a leadership position, felt more confident, and maintained a healthy lifestyle. Michael's transformation highlighted the power of affirmations in achieving personal and professional goals.

3. Sarah's Journey to Improved Relationships and Emotional Well-Being:

SARAH, A TEACHER, STRUGGLED with maintaining healthy relationships and managing stress. She felt disconnected from her loved ones and overwhelmed by her responsibilities. Determined to improve her relationships and emotional well-being, Sarah decided to use affirmations to foster positive changes.

Sarah's Affirmation Practice:

SARAH CREATED AFFIRMATIONS focused on relationships, emotional well-being, and self-care:

- "I build strong and meaningful connections with my family and friends."

- "I manage stress with confidence and maintain emotional well-being."

- "I prioritize self-care and make time for activities that bring me joy."

Steps Sarah Took:

1. MORNING RITUAL: Sarah started her day with affirmations while getting ready and during her morning commute.

2. Visualization: Sarah visualized herself building strong relationships, feeling connected and supported.

3. Self-Care Routine: Sarah established a self-care routine that included mindfulness practices, hobbies, and relaxation.

4. Seeking Support: Sarah sought support from a therapist and joined a support group for guidance and encouragement.

Sarah's Transformation:

THROUGH CONSISTENT affirmation practice and dedicated effort, Sarah improved her relationships and emotional well-being. She felt more connected to her loved ones, managed stress effectively, and prioritized self-care. Sarah's transformation highlighted the power of affirmations in fostering healthy relationships and emotional well-being.

4. David's Path to Financial Stability and Abundance:

DAVID, AN ENTREPRENEUR, faced financial challenges and struggled with managing his business finances. He felt overwhelmed by debt and uncertainty about his financial future. Determined to achieve financial stability and attract abundance, David decided to use affirmations to build confidence and stay motivated.

David's Affirmation Practice:

DAVID CREATED AFFIRMATIONS focused on financial stability, abundance, and confidence:

- "I am financially stable and manage my finances wisely."

- "I attract abundance and prosperity into my life."

- "I am confident in my ability to achieve financial security and success."

Steps David Took:

1. MORNING RITUAL: David started his day with affirmations while getting ready and during his morning commute.

2. Visualization: David visualized himself achieving financial stability, feeling secure and confident.

3. Financial Planning: David developed a detailed financial plan, including budgeting, saving, and debt repayment strategies.

4. Seeking Support: David sought advice from financial advisors and joined a business support group for guidance and encouragement.

David's Transformation:

THROUGH CONSISTENT affirmation practice and dedicated effort, David improved his financial situation and attracted abundance. He successfully managed his finances, reduced his debt, and achieved financial stability. David's transformation highlighted the power of affirmations in achieving financial goals and attracting prosperity.

Conclusion

Affirmations are powerful tools for creating a balanced and fulfilling life. By aligning your thoughts, beliefs, and actions with your values and goals, affirmations can help you achieve personal and professional success, build strong relationships, prioritize your health and well-being, and attract abundance.

In this chapter, we explored how to use affirmations to create a balanced and fulfilling life, integrate affirmations into all areas of your life, and shared real-life success stories of holistic transformation. By defining what fulfillment means to you, creating specific affirmations, integrating them into your daily routine, incorporating visualization and emotional engagement, and monitoring your progress, you can harness the power of affirmations to transform your life.

As you continue to practice affirmations and work towards your goals, remember to be patient and consistent. Positive change takes time, but with dedication and perseverance, you can harness the power of affirmations to create a balanced and fulfilling life. In the following chapters, we will explore specific areas where affirmations can make a significant impact, providing you with the tools and inspiration to harness the full potential of positive thinking.

Chapter 15: Sustaining the Affirmation Practice

Maintaining Long-Term Commitment to Affirmations

Embarking on the journey of using affirmations to enhance your life is a powerful step toward personal growth and fulfillment. However, sustaining this practice over the long term requires dedication, adaptability, and a commitment to continuous self-improvement. This chapter will explore strategies for maintaining a long-term commitment to affirmations, adapting and evolving your affirmations over time, and provide final words of encouragement to inspire continued growth.

Understanding the Importance of Long-Term Commitment:

AFFIRMATIONS ARE MOST effective when practiced consistently over time. Just like any other habit, the benefits of affirmations accumulate with sustained effort and regular practice. A long-term commitment to affirmations helps reinforce positive beliefs, align your actions with your goals, and foster a resilient and empowered mindset.

Challenges to Maintaining Long-Term Commitment:

WHILE THE BENEFITS of affirmations are clear, maintaining a long-term commitment can be challenging. Common obstacles include:

- Lack of Consistency: Inconsistent practice can undermine the effectiveness of affirmations.

- Diminished Motivation: Over time, initial enthusiasm may wane, leading to decreased motivation.

- External Distractions: Life's demands and distractions can interfere with regular practice.

- Skepticism: Doubts about the effectiveness of affirmations can hinder commitment.

- Stagnation: Using the same affirmations without evolution can lead to a sense of stagnation.

Steps for Maintaining Long-Term Commitment to Affirmations:

1. Establish a Routine:

CREATING A CONSISTENT routine is crucial for maintaining a long-term affirmation practice. Integrate affirmations into your daily schedule to ensure regular practice.

Steps for Establishing a Routine:

1. MORNING RITUAL: Start your day with affirmations to set a positive tone. Repeat them while getting ready, during your morning commute, or as part of your morning meditation.

2. Throughout the Day: Use reminders, such as sticky notes or phone alarms, to practice your affirmations throughout the day. Take short breaks to repeat your affirmations and refocus your mind.

3. Evening Reflection: End your day with affirmations to reinforce positive beliefs before sleep. Reflect on your goals and use affirmations to acknowledge your progress and commitment.

2. Keep a Progress Journal:

MAINTAINING A JOURNAL to track your progress, reflect on your experiences, and document your achievements can help you stay motivated and committed to your affirmation practice.

Steps for Keeping a Progress Journal:

1. SET REGULAR CHECK-Ins: Set aside regular times to reflect on your progress and update your journal. For example, "Every Sunday evening, I review my progress and update my journal."

2. Document Achievements: Record your achievements and milestones in your journal. For example, "This week, I successfully completed a major project at work and received positive feedback from my manager."

3. Reflect on Challenges: Reflect on any challenges you faced and how you overcame them. For example, "I faced a setback in my fitness routine, but I used affirmations to stay motivated and got back on track."

3. Celebrate Milestones and Achievements:

CELEBRATING YOUR MILESTONES and achievements can boost motivation and reinforce your commitment to your goals. Acknowledge your efforts and reward yourself for your progress.

Steps for Celebrating Milestones and Achievements:

1. SET MILESTONES: Break down your goals into smaller, manageable milestones. For example, "I will celebrate completing each chapter of my personal development book."

2. Acknowledge Your Efforts: Take time to acknowledge and celebrate your efforts and achievements. For example, "I am proud of my progress and celebrate my achievements with gratitude."

3. Reward Yourself: Reward yourself for reaching milestones and achieving goals. For example, "I will treat myself to a relaxing spa day after completing my certification course."

4. Stay Positive and Motivated:

MAINTAINING A POSITIVE mindset and staying motivated are crucial for achieving your goals. Use affirmations to reinforce your commitment, build confidence, and stay focused on your aspirations.

Steps for Staying Positive and Motivated:

1. USE POSITIVE AFFIRMATIONS: Regularly practice positive affirmations that reinforce your commitment and motivation. For example, "I am motivated and committed to achieving my goals."

2. Visualize Success: Visualize yourself achieving your goals and experiencing success. For example, "I see myself successfully completing my goals and feeling accomplished and fulfilled."

3. Practice Self-Compassion: Be kind and gentle with yourself, especially during setbacks. Use affirmations to practice self-compassion, such as "I am patient and understanding with myself as I navigate challenges."

5. Adjust Your Affirmation Plan as Needed:

FLEXIBILITY IS ESSENTIAL for staying on track and achieving your goals. Be open to adjusting your affirmation plan based on your progress and changing circumstances.

Steps for Adjusting Your Plan:

1. REGULARLY ASSESS Progress: Regularly assess your progress and determine if any adjustments are needed. For example, "Every month, I review my progress and adjust my plan if necessary."

2. Stay Flexible: Be open to making changes to your affirmation plan based on your needs and goals. For example, "I am flexible and adapt my plan to stay aligned with my goals."

3. Seek Feedback: Seek feedback from supportive individuals to gain insights and make informed adjustments. For example, "I seek feedback from my mentor to refine my affirmation plan and stay focused on my goals."

6. Seek Support and Accountability:

SHARING YOUR GOALS and affirmations with supportive friends, family members, or a mentor can provide encouragement and accountability. Consider joining a group or community focused on personal development to share experiences and gain insights.

Steps for Seeking Support and Accountability:

1. SHARE YOUR GOALS: Share your goals and affirmations with trusted individuals who can provide support and encouragement. For example, "I am working on improving my public speaking skills, and I use affirmations to build my confidence."

2. Join a Group: Consider joining a personal development group or online community to share experiences and gain insights. For example, "I am part of a personal development group where we share our goals and support each other's growth."

3. Seek a Mentor: Find a mentor who can provide guidance and accountability on your personal development journey. For example, "I have a mentor who helps me stay focused on my goals and provides valuable feedback."

Adapting and Evolving Your Affirmations Over Time

AS YOU PROGRESS ON your personal growth journey, your needs, goals, and circumstances may change. It's essential to adapt and evolve your affirmations to reflect these changes, ensuring that they remain relevant and impactful.

Understanding the Need for Adaptation:

ADAPTATION IS A NATURAL part of the growth process. As you achieve your goals and encounter new challenges, your affirmations should evolve to support your continued development and well-being.

Steps for Adapting and Evolving Your Affirmations:

1. Regularly Review and Update Your Affirmations:

REGULARLY REVIEWING and updating your affirmations ensures that they remain aligned with your current goals and aspirations. This helps maintain their relevance and effectiveness.

Steps for Reviewing and Updating Affirmations:

1. SET REGULAR REVIEW Intervals: Set aside regular times to review and update your affirmations. For example, "Every three months, I review my affirmations and update them as needed."

2. Assess Alignment with Goals: Assess whether your current affirmations align with your current goals and aspirations. For example, "I review my affirmations to ensure they support my goals for personal growth and career advancement."

3. Update Affirmations: Update your affirmations to reflect any changes in your goals or circumstances. For example, "I update my affirmations to focus on my new goal of starting my own business."

2. Create New Affirmations for Emerging Goals:

AS YOU ACHIEVE YOUR current goals, you may set new goals and aspirations. Create new affirmations to support these emerging goals, ensuring that they align with your values and priorities.

Steps for Creating New Affirmations:

1. IDENTIFY NEW GOALS: Reflect on your progress and identify any new goals or aspirations. For example, "I want to develop new skills and expand my knowledge in a different field."

2. Create Specific Affirmations: Create specific affirmations that support your new goals. For example, "I am dedicated to learning new skills and expanding my knowledge in my chosen field."

3. Integrate New Affirmations: Integrate your new affirmations into your daily routine, ensuring they receive the same focus and attention as your existing affirmations.

3. Reflect on Your Growth and Evolution:

REGULARLY REFLECTING on your growth and evolution helps you stay connected to your personal development journey and appreciate the progress you've made. This reflection can inspire new affirmations and reinforce your commitment to continuous growth.

Steps for Reflecting on Growth and Evolution:

1. SET REFLECTION INTERVALS: Set aside regular times to reflect on your growth and evolution. For example, "Every six months, I reflect on my personal growth and the progress I've made."

2. Celebrate Achievements: Acknowledge and celebrate your achievements and milestones. For example, "I celebrate my progress in developing new skills and achieving my career goals."

3. Identify Areas for Further Growth: Reflect on areas where you want to continue growing and evolving. For example, "I want to continue developing my leadership skills and building stronger relationships."

4. Seek Continuous Learning and Development:

EMBRACE A MINDSET OF continuous learning and development. Seek opportunities to expand your knowledge, develop new skills, and explore new interests. This ongoing growth will inspire new affirmations and support your long-term commitment to personal development.

Steps for Seeking Continuous Learning and Development:

1. Read Books: Read books on personal development, self-improvement, and subjects that interest you. Use affirmations to reinforce your love of learning, such as "I am committed to continuous learning and personal development."

2. Attend Workshops and Seminars: Attend workshops, seminars, or online courses to gain practical insights and strategies. Use affirmations to stay motivated, such as "I am open to new opportunities for growth and learning."

3. Engage in New Experiences: Seek out new experiences that challenge you and help you grow. Use affirmations to build confidence in your ability to embrace new experiences, such as "I embrace new experiences with confidence and curiosity."

5. Stay Open to Feedback and Growth:

EMBRACE FEEDBACK AS an opportunity for growth. Seek input from others to gain new perspectives and insights that can enhance your affirmation practice and personal development journey.

Steps for Staying Open to Feedback and Growth:

1. SEEK CONSTRUCTIVE Feedback: Actively seek constructive feedback from trusted friends, family members, mentors, or colleagues. For example, "I seek feedback from my mentor to gain insights on how to improve my leadership skills."

2. Reflect on Feedback: Reflect on the feedback you receive and identify areas for growth and improvement. For example, "I reflect on the feedback I received and identify ways to enhance my communication skills."

3. Incorporate Feedback into Your Practice: Use the feedback to refine your affirmation practice and personal development goals. For example, "I update my affirmations to focus on improving my communication skills and building stronger relationships."

Final Words of Encouragement and Continued Growth

EMBARKING ON THE JOURNEY of using affirmations to enhance your life is a powerful step toward personal growth and fulfillment. As you continue this journey, remember that the key to sustained success lies in your commitment, adaptability, and willingness to embrace continuous growth.

Embrace the Journey:

PERSONAL GROWTH AND development are lifelong journeys filled with opportunities for learning, self-discovery, and transformation. Embrace this journey with an open heart and a positive mindset, knowing that each step brings you closer to your goals and aspirations.

Stay Patient and Persistent:

POSITIVE CHANGE TAKES time, and progress may not always be linear. Stay patient and persistent, trusting in the process and your ability to achieve your goals. Remember that setbacks are opportunities for growth, and each challenge you overcome strengthens your resilience and determination.

Celebrate Your Progress:

TAKE TIME TO CELEBRATE your progress and achievements, no matter how small they may seem. Acknowledging your efforts and successes reinforces your commitment and motivates you to continue striving for your goals.

Celebrate each milestone with gratitude and pride, knowing that you are moving forward on your personal growth journey.

Cultivate a Growth Mindset:

A GROWTH MINDSET IS the belief that your abilities and intelligence can be developed through dedication, effort, and continuous learning. Cultivate this mindset by embracing challenges, seeking opportunities for growth, and viewing setbacks as opportunities for improvement. Use affirmations to reinforce your growth mindset, such as "I embrace challenges as opportunities for growth and learning."

Surround Yourself with Support:

SURROUND YOURSELF WITH supportive individuals who encourage and inspire you on your personal growth journey. Share your goals and affirmations with trusted friends, family members, or a mentor who can provide guidance and accountability. Consider joining a community or group focused on personal development to share experiences and gain insights.

Practice Self-Compassion:

BE KIND AND GENTLE with yourself, especially during challenging times. Practice self-compassion by acknowledging your efforts and treating yourself with the same kindness and understanding that you would offer to a friend. Use affirmations to practice self-compassion, such as "I am kind and gentle with myself as I navigate challenges."

Stay Open to Growth and Change:

EMBRACE A MINDSET OF continuous growth and change. Stay open to new experiences, opportunities, and feedback that can enhance your personal development journey. Remember that growth is a dynamic process, and your affirmations and goals may evolve as you progress.

Final Words of Encouragement:

AS YOU CONTINUE YOUR affirmation practice and personal growth journey, remember that you have the power to create a fulfilling and purposeful life. Your thoughts, beliefs, and actions shape your reality, and by aligning them with your deepest values and aspirations, you can achieve your goals and realize your potential.

Stay committed to your practice, embrace the journey with an open heart, and celebrate your progress along the way. You are capable of achieving great things, and with dedication and perseverance, you can harness the power of affirmations to transform your life.

Continued Growth:

YOUR JOURNEY OF PERSONAL growth and development is ongoing, and each step brings you closer to your goals and aspirations. Continue to seek opportunities for learning, embrace challenges with confidence, and stay committed to your affirmation practice. With each passing day, you are becoming the best version of yourself, and your efforts are creating a life filled with joy, purpose, and fulfillment.

Don't miss out!

Visit the website below and you can sign up to receive emails whenever Timothy Scott Phillips publishes a new book. There's no charge and no obligation.

https://books2read.com/r/B-A-KCQWC-MCGJF

BOOKS 2 READ

Connecting independent readers to independent writers.

About the Author

Timothy Scott Phillips is a dedicated author specializing in non-fiction self-help books that empower readers to overcome challenges and embrace personal growth. With a passion for mental health, resilience, and self-improvement, Timothy combines research-based insights with practical strategies to inspire lasting change. His work reflects a deep commitment to helping individuals navigate life's complexities, build confidence, and unlock their full potential. When he's not writing, Timothy enjoys mentoring, exploring nature, and connecting with his readers to share stories of transformation and hope. His books are a testament to the power of perseverance and the human spirit.

www.ingramcontent.com/pod-product-compliance
Lightning Source LLC
LaVergne TN
LVHW041211150826
845673LV00001B/356

* 9 7 9 8 2 3 0 1 4 1 9 1 4 *